D0200766

Property of
HOLSUM BAKERY, INC
Phoenix, AZ

Property of
HOLSUM BAKERY, INC.
Phoenix, AZ

WINNING THE WAR ON WASTE:
CHANGING THE WAY WE WORK
WILLIAM E. CONWAY

Property of
HOLSUM BAKERY, INC.
Phoenix, AZ

Conway Quality, Inc.
15 Trafalgar Square
Nashua, NH 03063
1-800-359-0099

Winning The War On Waste: Changing The Way We Work.
Copyright 1996 by William E. Conway. All rights reserved.

First Edition Copyright 1994 Conway Quality, Inc.

Printed in the United States of America. No part of this book may
be used or reproduced in any manner whatsoever without written
permission except in the case of brief quotations embodied in
critical articles or reviews.

International Standard Book Number 0-9631464-4-0
Library of Congress Catalog Card Number 94-094130

Conway Quality, Inc
15 Trafalgar Square
Nashua, NH 03063
Tel: 1-603-889-1130
Fax: 1-603-889-0033

10   9   8   7   6   5   4   3   2

DEDICATION

This book is dedicated to Dr. W. Edwards Deming, whose ideas serve as the basis for the system of continuous improvement through the elimination of waste.

My education in this new paradigm of management began in March of 1979, the day I met Dr. Deming. Shortly thereafter he began working with me and many others in my organization, first to convince, then educate, and finally help us convert his ideas into a practical plan for continuous improvement. I worked closely with him for four years, and every time we met, I gained some new insight into how his ideas could be applied.

His stature in Japan is much greater than it is in the U.S. There he is revered. This is because his ideas have been so widely used to help in making Japan a world-class competitor in many industries. At Toyota headquaters, the lobby has three pictures— one of the company's founder, another of the current chairman and the largest one is of Dr. Deming. The Deming Prize, awarded to companies who most successfully follow his principles, is the most sought after award in Japanese industry.

The people at Conway Quality and I converted the theories, principles, and 14 points of Dr. Deming into a practical way to run a business or a department.

Over the years since I founded Conway Quality I carried on an extensive correspondence with Dr. Deming, and he was always generous with his time, and thoughtful in his writing.

I, along with a great many organizations throughout the world, owe him much and respect him greatly. For that reason, I dedicate this book to the memory of Dr. W. Edwards Deming—the "Father of the Third Wave of the Industrial Revolution."

Property of HOLSUM BAKERY, INC. Phoenix, AZ

ACKNOWLEDGMENTS

The ideas and techniques for the new system of continuous improvement are evolving. Continuous improvement applies to the system of continuous improvement itself as it does to anything else. The ideas come from everyone I contact, particularly the clients of Conway Quality, Inc. The ideas are brought together and distilled by the people of Conway Quality. These clients and people are the ones that deserve the most credit for this book.

I would like to thank Lawrence C. Hornor for assistance in writing, Brock Dethier for his editorial assistance, and Curtis King for coordinating the whole endeavor.

Finally, I would like to recognize the significant contributions to the book made by Don Brown, Jim Copley, Jody Gunnerson, Mary Jane King and Bob Potter, Senior Associates at Conway Quality. In particular, Bob Potter was a major contributor to the sections on Major Management Innovations and Erik Riswick, President of Ready Bake Division of Weston Foods Ltd., made many important suggestions.

TABLE OF CONTENTS

FORWARD
BY LARRY C. HORNOR

Bill Conway first began working with Dr. W. Edwards Deming in 1979. Since that time, quality management systems based on Dr. Deming's teachings have spread throughout the Western world. Conway Quality, Inc. and several other companies teach the practical application of Dr. Deming's principles. Many organizations have benefited greatly, while others mount an effort for a while but "just don't get it" and abandon their endeavor.

While working with Bill and his clients I have found that people have difficulty knowing just what steps to take in their organization to get things rolling. Recently, I had lunch with an executive who was attending one of Bill's seminars. He began to tell me what he really needed to move forward with Continuous Improvement. It came down to four basics.

One, he needed something that gave him a better understanding of how Bill led the process of change, and how that can apply in other situations. Two, he wanted to know in detail just what to do to analyze the work and find and eliminate the waste. Three, he wanted some more guidance about establishing projects, project objectives and project teams. Finally, he wanted to know just how to go about educating and training himself and the people who worked with him and for him.

I repeated all of this to Bill when he returned from a trip about a week later. Out of that conversation this book was born. As the book evolved, Bill added sections about how to plan the quality effort, how to treat people and how to work with customers and suppliers.

This book provides the help to people who want to join the quality revolution and are looking for practical information on just what to do and how to do it.

INTRODUCTION: WHY READ THIS BOOK?

The purpose of this book is to help anyone, at any level, in any area of their organization, to do the following:

- Motivate themselves to do much more—both as a leader and as a participant in improving themselves and their organization
- Understand and learn what to do and how to do it
- Carry out what they have learned.

Regardless of where you and your organization now stand, this book will be a major help to you.

The Quality Revolution really started in war manufacturing industries in the United States during World War II. Dr. W. Edwards Deming and others helped people in these industries to study the work and work processes to increase production, raise quality and reliability levels, reduce time to do anything, reduce costs and improve productivity. Due to the lack of top management involvement and understanding of these efforts, however, the revolution had practically died in the United States by 1950. The revolution started again in post-war Japan in 1950, and has returned to the western world where it has begun to take hold, but at far too slow a pace. Companies such as Hewlett Packard, Dow Chemical, and Motorola, leaders in commerce and industry, recognize the rewards of following this management technology.

Why then has implementation of these principles in the Western world been so slow and halting? The quality revolution has been so gradual in the West primarily because of the major change in management thinking required. Most Western managers don't understand quality; they haven't been willing to invest the time necessary to learn about the revolution, and consequently most of the people who should be leading the revolution lack the commitment that is crucial to the success of the new way of working. Many people do not understand that quality of the final product or service is not, by itself, enough. IBM and General Motors produce quality products and services, but because they didn't arrive at quality in the right way, they have been struggling. The quality revolution is about the way to run the business or the organization at every level in every area. It is what to work on, how to price, how to purchase, how to develop the strategic plan, reduce costs, sell more, develop new products, and treat people. The system encompasses everything not just manufacturing. Key parts of this new management system are expanding the business and creating jobs. Many organizations that claim to be working "in quality" are neither growing their businesses nor creating jobs.

The Quality Secret is that you can simultaneously achieve high quality and low cost through a continual, pervasive effort to identify and eliminate waste in all work and work processes. This effort yields consistently high-quality products and services that meet or exceed external customers' requirements at low cost and expense. Working on the right things at every level of the organization, combined with close attention to customer wants and needs, insures a competitive or even world-class organization and usually leads to profitable growth of the enterprise.

A continual effort to eliminate waste means continuous change. It means involving, motivating, and using the brains, time and energy of all the people in the organization. If they are to work for quality, the people must share a desire for continuous improvement. Continuous improvement includes innovation and reengineering as well as incremental change. This is a major challenge for the organization's leadership.

What we call the core activity is to identify, quantify and eliminate waste through continuous process improvement. Note that the key step is to identify and quantify the waste and then identify the *processes* to change or improve to eliminate that waste. That is quite different from simply searching for processes to improve and then improving those processes. It is also quite different from merely turning out a quality product or service. This search for waste examines all processes—those in strategic planning, marketing, sales, distribution, product development, administration, legal services, manufacturing, health care, financial services, etc.

Even those people who understand what the continuous improvement system is all about and want to adopt it often don't understand what specific steps to take. The purpose of my first book, *The Quality Secret*, was to explain the system in a practical manner and generate a strong desire in the reader to adopt its principles. This more detailed book shows what specific steps to take to create a world class organization which will compete effectively in the 1990's and beyond.

Although top level managers have the best opportunity to bring about major change, people at all levels can make changes in their areas and influence their peers to contribute. So this book is for all those people who wish to learn how to make substantial improvement in operations and plans.

GET READY FOR CHANGE

While learning what to do is simple, transforming the management system usually is difficult. For most people, working the new way requires a complete change in thinking, a new paradigm or model of how things are done. To have continuous improvement there has to be continual change.

But the continuous improvement system does work. It can dramatically reduce the time to do anything. It improves the quality of products and services to please external customers while at the same time reducing costs. The results are often dramatic. It has been proven effective over and over by organizations that really work the new way. It can also fail. Because change is difficult, a lack of education, training, leadership or overall commitment will bring failure. The leader's job is to bring about the necessary change in outlook, to lead others to embrace continuous improvement as their primary job, and to provide the necessary resources, including education and training, to help people implement the continuous improvement system.

WHAT THIS BOOK OFFERS

All people in an organization—from the person answering the telephone in the office or doing a repetitive task on an assembly line, to the chief executive—can improve their work by applying the principles and methods contained in this book. But because the quality revolution can succeed totally *only* with the leadership of top managers, the people who make the decision to work the new way, I have addressed much of this book directly to management. However, all people in the organization should read this book since all can contribute importantly to improving the work processes.

I divide improvement projects into two basic kinds: 1) those major process changes which must be initiated and led by top management and 2) those improvements which can be led by others in the organization. The triangle below shows these two types with the level of leadership as the key difference between them.

Continuous Improvement

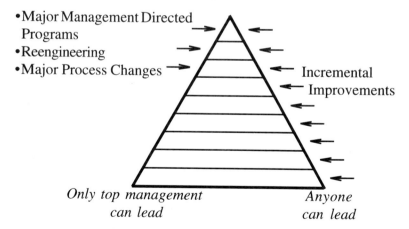

• Major Management Directed Programs
• Reengineering
• Major Process Changes

Incremental Improvements

Only top management can lead

Anyone can lead

On the right side, the improvements include individual projects, team projects contained within one department and most larger projects involving two or more departments (cross-department projects). Anyone at the appropriate level can lead these projects.

The left side depicts "Major Management Innovations. These are changes that will have such affect on the organization and/or require such major resources that they can only be led by top management. Today these changes are often called "Reengineering". It is important to understand that continuous improvement is a state of mind that should permeate all levels of the organization.

As you read the first chapter, "Lead the Revolution," I hope you become excited by the successes of other leaders and motivated to act in your own organization. The chapter explains a number of key concepts of continuous improvement, and it includes real-world cases that demonstrate how applying each concept, leading in the new way, paid off for a particular organization. Someone who reads only the first chapter would have a pretty good sense of what this revolution is about and how to begin leading it.

The second chapter, "Educate and Act," introduces the core activity of continuous improvement, begins the discussion of finding the waste and making major changes, and outlines the kinds of education and training most people need before they can work in the new way. (Appendix C contains a full discussion of education and training programs.) Expanding on a concept explored in the first part of chapter 1, this chapter encourages you to move people into action quickly, because successful action creates joy in achievement that leads to motivation.

"Plan, Promote, and Assess," the third chapter, explains how to assess where the organization is and where it wants to go. It leads you through a detailed assessment of the current situation of a company, helping you to see how you can assess your own organization.

Though Chapter 4, "Choose the Vital Few," is short, it is essential for anyone wanting to bring about major improvements in quality, efficiency, or profitability. It emphasizes that the most important decision is the first one: What do we work on? And it shows how your answer to that question should guide your definition of a mission and vision and creation of the first continuous improvement programs and projects.

Chapter 5, "Organize Projects," details how to set up teams that will root out the waste and gives numerous examples of the kind of projects that such teams can successfully pursue.

Chapter 6, "Major Management Innovations," describes how reengineering is one part of continuous improvement. It provides clues to help identify reengineering opportunities and keys to success.

Chapter 7, "Analyze Work and Eliminate Waste," briefly explains the key concepts and tools used to find and eliminate waste.

Chapters 8, and 9 explain how relationships with all the people inside the organization and with customers and suppliers outside the organization need to change for continuous improvement to be successful. You cannot afford to overlook these issues, for leaders cannot hope to introduce continuous improvement without the commitment of the people around them any more than the people can make major changes without a committed leader. Continuous improvement involves all the people and all the processes of the organization.

Chapter 10 suggests how to keep improving on into the future. The five appendices give detailed advice about how to develop the continuous improvement attitude, how to educate and train people to work the new way, and how to perform work sampling and make flow charts.

As a whole, this book offers the most complete guide available to implementing the quality revolution. After reading it, you will know not just what changes are needed and why they are necessary, but what to do Monday morning, next week, and next month to improve the quality of your work processes and therefore please your customers and become more competitive. It's hard to truly understand and appreciate the importance and the benefits of continuous improvement until you begin taking action. This book should give you the motivation to get started and the concepts and techniques you will need to succeed. If started, as most organizations have done, you will be ready to re-group and move to new, larger and more pervasive levels of understanding and activity. Use this book to move to be the best in your industry.

Those people in organizations that have been working in Quality Management (TQM, Continuous Improvement) for years should pay special attention to the following areas:

- Importance of the use of the concept of waste (the Core Activity) by everyone to determine where to work
- How to use the Value Added concept to make huge and continual improvements
- Concentration on meeting the needs of external customers rather than internal customers (meet wants and needs of internal customers that are also in the interest of external customers)
- Need for continual leadership everywhere
- How to integrate Major Management Innovation into continuous improvement

Winning the War on Waste should be used at every level by the managers in working with their people. For example each week or month, the team reads a chapter and then meets for 1 to 4 hours to review what they learned, and what new or added things they should do. In other words, use this book, along with *The Quality Secret*, to regenerate your activities as a leader for real Quality Management.

CHAPTER 1
LEAD THE REVOLUTION

How do you lead people in the quality revolution? First and foremost, what is it all about? There has been a revolution in work through quality—both in what we work on and the way we work. In my first book, *The Quality Secret*, and our seminar and videos we call it The Right Way To Manage©. It is continuous improvement...forever. It is a management system—the way we think, talk, work, and act. Our task as leaders at any level is to make working this new way the only acceptable way. We achieve this by leading, not by ordering. As much as possible, we want the desire to work this new way to be intrinsic.

Below we have the Core Activity and the four main supporting elements to work this new way. The core activity is to identify, quantify and eliminate waste through continuous process improvement. The waste is in every form of material, capital, time to do anything including the time of people and all the lost sales and lost opportunities. This waste often reaches 30 to 40% of revenue. Most people will find this hard to believe so let me repeat, this waste often reaches 30 to 40% of revenue.

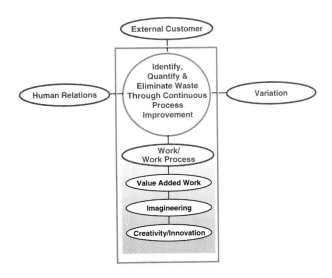

The four main supporting elements are the following:

- External customers who pay the bill and/or use the product or service—"no customers, no orders, no jobs".
- Human relations—including treating people as you would like to be treated and working together, lifting people up to raise the average, and make it in everyone's interest to do the core activity.
- Variation, the technical tool we use to help us find the waste—the troubles, problems, errors, complexities, wastes and opportunities—and to track the waste down and make the improvements.
- The study, change and improvement of the work and work process using the industrial engineering principles and the concept of value added work.

Having a balance between these elements is key. There are lots of organizations that please customers so much that they go out of business. Everyone can be happy and still go out of business. Everyone can have charts and still have disastrous performance. Remember that we must study, change and improve work and the work process to get rid of the waste. If we do not do that, all is lost.

That is what we will do to "Lead the Revolution." Leadership is not based on personality traits or the charisma of a "natural" leader. Although those things may help, leadership requires the right attitudes and behaviors. Success requires leaders who strongly and sincerely desire continuous improvement, who respect the organization's people, and who refuse to tolerate waste. But that is not enough.

This chapter presents a number of cases that demonstrate the importance of leadership in the new system. I have chosen the cases both to exemplify the key leadership activities (summarized by the headings) and to motivate you to lead the quality revolution that I have detailed in the rest of the book. Each case shows how intervention--usually by a top manager or outsider--led to measurable, lasting, positive change. As you read these cases, think about the similar actions that you could take and imagine the rewards for you and your organization.

To be successful, projects to improve work and eliminate waste must take place at all levels of the organization. However, working in the new way should start at the top. Top management should provide the innovation, resources and support needed for any major changes to work processes affecting all, or a large part, of the organization. I call these major management innovations. These major projects are also referred to as reengineering. Most of the following cases (except for the first) are major process changes and thus are major management innovations. These major projects normally generate many sub projects and sub-sub projects, etc. These sub projects generally fall into three categories:

- Substantial projects involving two or more departments
- Projects contained within one department
- Individual projects

These projects may be initiated at any level, or they may be created as sub-projects of a major management innovation. These levels of projects are described more fully in Chapter 6.

MOVE PEOPLE INTO ACTION

Because this system is new and different to most people, motivation by convincing or telling people to "get on board" is usually ineffective. In fact, the conventional cycle of

Motivation—>Action—>Achievement

does not work for most major changes in attitude. Move people into action first and then show them what they can achieve. Then the joy and satisfaction of that achievement will provide the motivation for further action. Thus, the new cycle is:

Action—>Achievement—>Motivation—>Action—>

I have seen this practical way to motivate people succeed throughout my career. When it came to changing the management system
to one of continuous improvement we used the same approach—
we moved people to action working in the new way. Quickly
people felt the joy of achievement, and that led to motivation. Then
they took further action.

In working with many organizations for the last ten years, I
have seen leaders who think that they must motivate the people.
They work on the motivation, focusing primarily on human relations
first. While I would not want to overlook any aspect of human
relations as we start working the new way, I believe strongly that
the way to help people is to move them into action. When the action
leads to achievement, motivation will follow. Seeing the results of
action is the best motivator.

Case: The Entertainment Center

A few years ago, my wife and I bought a new television, a
VCR, a stereo system, a CD player, and an entertainment center
to put them in. We soon had the new electronic components
working, but the entertainment center itself sat in the garage in its
box, week after week. Everything was working fine as far as I was
concerned, and it began to look as though the entertainment center
would stay in the garage forever. Every now and then my wife or
one of my children would suggest that we should get the entertainment center out of its box and set it up, but we always seemed to
put it off. We weren't motivated enough to get started.

Then one Sunday, my daughter-in-law, Ann, my son, Jim, and
their three children arrived for a regular visit. When they came in
the door, Ann said, "Today's the day!"

I said, "What do you mean, today's the day?"

"Today is the day we put the entertainment center together!"

"Oh no!" I said, starting to think of all the reasons we
couldn't do it today.

But already Jim had the center on a dolly and was hauling it up the steps into the living room. They opened up the big carton and put the pieces of oak all over the floor of three rooms. Ann handed me the instructions to put it together.

She said, "You're the boss. You're in charge, you have the instructions, you tell us who does what, when to do it, and, if necessary, how to do it. Get us started now."

I started reading the instructions and thought, "Oh no, what am I into now?" I got out the hardware--all the screws and the nuts with different lengths, shapes and sizes. I got out the right screwdrivers and said to my grandson, "Jay, you're responsible for the hardware. You give out the material. You make sure that we measure the screw size against the picture we have here in the instructions."

Jay agreed, and we started. We read the instructions and started to put it together. To our surprise, the instructions were outstanding. We didn't have any trouble at all. We had to stop and study a few times, but for the most part we put the entertainment center together smoothly. About two hours later there it was— every piece of the entertainment center was in place in the den. We hooked up the wires, moved the electronic equipment in, and by two hours and a half it was done and everything was working.

I said to my daughter-in-law, "Ann, I saw what you did."

She said, "What do you mean?"

"I saw how you moved us all into action. Once we took the first steps successfully, we were motivated to work more."

She said, "That's the way, Bill."

Drawing upon her background as a psychiatric social worker, Ann said, "Bill, anyone who understands the human mind knows the best way to motivate people is to move them into action. They do it, feel the joy of achievement, and get motivated to do more. That's the way it works, Bill."

A few days later, she brought a textbook that confirmed our observations: action leads to achievement, then to motivation, and motivation to more action and more achievement and motivation.

CHANGE PEOPLE'S ATTITUDES

To work in the new way, with continuous improvement as the goal, most people need to change their attitudes dramatically. Everyone needs to believe in continuous improvement, respect their colleagues at all levels of the organization's hierarchy, and develop an intolerance for waste. To motivate these changes in attitude, the organization as a whole must be dissatisfied with the present situation, become aware of a better system, and develop the know-how to implement the new system. If employees, or worse, top management are satisfied with the status quo, it will be very difficult to implement the new system. Leaders of the organization may confront some serious obstacles to adopting the new attitudes, so changing people's attitudes is a major leadership task.

It is difficult to change people's attitudes by telling them, or even persuading them. To change their basic attitude, people need to *experience* the new system working. When I first tried to get people to change, the resistance was monumental. First, people did not understand what I was talking about. After a substantial period of education and training, most began to understand on an intellectual level, but they still did not think it was worth the effort. I talked about it continually at all levels, inquiring, cajoling and helping people to move into action. Still the initial reaction from most was lip service.

Fortunately, some people moved into action. Whether they were convinced in their own minds, tried it on faith, or did it because that was what the boss wanted, I still am not sure. Whenever someone seemed to be responding by taking action, I helped in every way I could. Results create momentum.

Case: Momentum Builds on Success

The first large success at Nashua Corporation was in a major manufacturing operation which coated a specialty paper. A project using the continuous improvement system improved quality and consistency, increased output, and saved hundreds of thousands of dollars. In addition, the improved quality of our product helped us increase sales and gain new customers. We publicized this success throughout the company, and we recognized the people involved in the project. Their achievement motivated them to continue to search for improvements throughout their operation. Slowly, others decided to take action. Not all projects were successful, but a number of small and large projects began to show results. The momentum built.

I told people that future evaluations of their performance would be based substantially on whether or how they actively embraced the continuous improvement system. Gradually it became known that the only acceptable way of acting was to work in the new way.

Encouragement and help are sufficient to move most people into action. But seeing results, experiencing achievement, is the only way to get a permanent change in attitude and behavior. How large a group you can lead into action is somewhat dependent on your position in the organization. There can be leaders at all levels, because people can influence their peers, and sometimes their boss. To make a large, permanent change, the leaders have to be well up in the organization, ideally at the top. Top management not only has more influence, but also can marshal the resources needed for education, training and action. Those working *on* the system should provide coaching and support for those working *in* the system.

MOTIVATE AT EVERY LEVEL

Of course, if you have a large organization, you cannot be the only leader moving people into action, working the new way. Training people, providing them with the right tools, moving them into action, and giving them a taste of the joy of achievement motivates people, and their enthusiasm is contagious from one level of the organization to the next.

Case: Lost Sales at Nashua Copycat

Jim Copley, who at that time was General Manager of our Office Products Division at Nashua Corporation, had responsibility for our European distribution of office copy machines. I had worked with Jim to find and attack the waste in the domestic business. He decided to take what he had learned and apply it in the United Kingdom. The job of our U. K. subsidiary, Nashua Copycat, Ltd., was to build a successful growth business selling copy machines, service and supplies. We wanted to gain market share, create jobs and make more money. Many people believe that quality management does not apply to the sales area. But if you look at sales by focusing on waste, you will find that you can usually apply quality principles to sales more profitably than to any other area. Jim knew of the many other ways to sell more. In the previous year, there had been work done to improve the "people selection process" and to train the sales people more effectively. Jim and others were already hard at work to improve sales productivity through new and improved products and services That was planned for one year later. Jim also had work started on improved lead generation processes which came to fruition 6-9 months later. In the case of Nashua Copycat, a key to finding the waste at this time was work sampling.

At Nashua Copycat the activity that drove all the others was the sale or lease of copy machines by our extensive sales staff. When Jim got there, he called all the managers together and readily got their agreement that their most important job was to find all the troubles and problems that prevented the salespeople from being as efficient and effective as possible in placing copy machines.

They then went through the process of making a sale:

- Generate leads
    - Cold Call
    - Advertising
    - Other

- Call lead and try for appointment
- Visit lead and arrange demonstration
- Give demonstration and arrange trial or close sale
- Convert trials to sales
- Bring back information on other customer needs and wants

After much discussion they agreed that these were the activities that supported their mission of placing copy machines. Jim asked people to gather data that would help to answer important questions such as what type of lead resulted in the most sales, how many leads a salesperson could effectively handle in a week and how many cold calls were equivalent to one lead.

Then Jim asked each of the managers to estimate what percentage of their salespeople's time was spent on the activities listed, which all agreed were what the salespeople should be doing. Their estimates ranged from 65% to 85% and averaged 70%.

Jim said "Why don't we find out? I need a volunteer." Brian, the sales manager for suburban London, volunteered. He had estimated that his sales people were spending 70% of their time on the listed activities. Jim worked with him and explained how to help the sales people do work sampling. Jim said, "I'm going to provide an industrial engineer to help you do the work sampling studies. Then in four weeks we'll go over the results of your study and see what we can learn."

Four weeks later, when the managers had gathered again, Brian presented his results. He said, "I still can't believe it, but my salespeople are spending only 29% of their time on the things that count!" Then they went over all the things that they were doing that didn't count—traveling, handling customer complaints, scheduling service calls, explaining invoices, expediting deliveries of supplies, trying to collect accounts receivable, hunting for leads for which they had the wrong address, attending sales meetings, filling out forms, etc. Brian then showed a Pareto chart of the non-productive activities, and travel time was the biggest one.

Non-Productive Activities of Salespeople

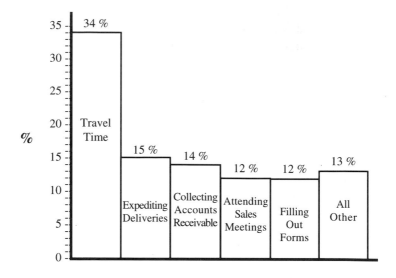

Brian had already figured out that no one, including the salesperson, was planning the travel. Leads were handed out at random every day, and they were generally scattered all over the territory. Brian figured that with a little planning, he could cut the travel time by 40%. The group then discussed all the other non-productive activities and ways to reduce or eliminate them.

The data made it apparent that cold calls were ineffective, since it took 12 cold calls to equal one good lead. They discussed ways of getting more leads and more effective leads.

The group made assignments, and over the next seven months, machine placements per salesperson per month increased 52%! As people saw the improvements, they became more and more enthusiastic. Since the salespeople were partly paid on commission, they were the most enthusiastic of all. They contributed many ideas for improving their use of time and were proud of their increase in sales. Gradually, as the group eliminated the troubles and problems, market share and profitability rose dramatically, and surveys showed that customer satisfaction also increased. Despite big improvements in quality and productivity, we needed more people.

Because achievement brought motivation, working the new way spread quickly throughout the organization. To change the culture, nothing is more effective than showing people that it can work. Then move them into action and joy of achievement will provide the motivation for change and further action. Every enthusiastic convert to the new system becomes a leader for change. And in this case, leadership and careful work sampling created the converts. This brought about major changes in the work processes including the heavy use of computerized information to help everyone. The leads and the follow up system for all sales people brought about dramatic improvements with sales rising over 50% in the following 6 months.

SPREAD THE WORD

The concept of continuous improvement and the motivation to work on it spreads best if a top leader begins the work and enlists the people reporting to him or her. They in turn enlist their people, and the new way branches out through the organization. Below is an inverted tree—it represents how most organizations operate.

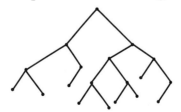

If there is a blockage at any level of the organization, it is not likely that much will happen with the branches (people) below that level. I'll never forget what Dr. Deming told us on the first day we met with him, March 9, 1979: "Bill, you will be the leader of the change. You will see that the six Vice Presidents sitting at the meeting with you will be the leaders of the change in their areas. You will see that each one of these V.P.'s provides leadership, level by level, for the people throughout the organization."

It's very easy to see where the behavior breaks down when you interview people level by level in different areas. And once you see the break, you'll discover that most of the people below the break point don't do much in the new way. They're looking above them for the example.

Obviously the most desirable way to spread the new behavior throughout the organization is level by level, as Dr. Deming specified. Each person helps the people below him or her to understand the new system of management and to bring about continuous improvement.

Sometimes, however, someone in senior management "just doesn't get it," even though that person is trying to work the new way. In this case, with the knowledge and permission of the person involved, a top executive can sometimes work directly with someone lower in the organization to get a demonstration project started and show what can be done.

Case: The President Steps In

The President of a company wanted to help the financial/ administrative part of the company practice The Right Way To Manage. The Vice-President of Finance, the Treasurer, the Controller, and numerous managers and supervisors had been trained in the simple statistical tools and problem solving. Many had been exposed in some depth to statistical process control, imagineering, surveys, and principles of work. Charts were everywhere. They had completed a few good projects and were holding meetings on quality at all levels. Quality circle activity at lower levels was spotty. All kinds of human relations activities were in place to encourage continuous improvement.

On a visit to the V. P. of Finance, the President commented that very few large gains were being achieved in the Financial/ Administrative area and that much greater effort and progress were needed to make continuous improvements in the quality and productivity of *all* work. The V. P. said he knew that and he wanted progress but he and the other managers did not know what else to do or how to do it. They were doing the best that they could. Everyone had projects and charts. The President volunteered to talk directly with some department heads to see if he could help. The V. P. told him to go ahead—he wanted the help.

A short time later, the President met with the Payroll Manager to discuss the Payroll Department activities in making continuous improvements in the quality and productivity of *all* work. The office of the Payroll Manager was wall-to-wall with charts. As the Payroll Manager described each chart and the reason for it, the President could see that few, if any, significant improvements were underway.

The following conversation then took place:

Pres: "How many people do you have?"

Mgr: "Six."

Pres: "Six! What do they do?

Mgr: "It's a big job! We pay 4,000 people all over the USA in 8 plants and 25 sales offices. We do a great job, pay everyone the right amount, pay them on the right day and hardly ever receive a complaint."

Pres: "With modern data processing I would think that one person could do it. What is the work anyway?

Mgr: "Enter the payroll data; provide data to the Personnel Department and others for fringe benefit information; handle special queries; and see that people get accurate checks on time. Just entering the data is a big job with 4,000 people coming and going, changing jobs, etc."

Pres: "How much work is it for data entry?"

Mgr: (After investigating with his six people) "Half a person—20 hours per week."

Pres: "Great, one half down, 5 1/2 to go! What is the rest?"

Mgr: "Well everything is all screwed up. Henry over there in the Traffic Department—he's been here 40 years— no one likes to cross him. Every week his data is all messed up—we have to double check everything. And the California Plant Manager—she reports to the General Manager, then to a Vice-President, a group Vice President, and finally to you! Her stuff is just a mess. Faxes, letters, telephone calls, personal visits— the mistakes and work go on and on. It's the same thing with the Dallas Sales Office, Georgia Plant, Chicago and Miami offices, all over the place."

Pres: "How much time is that?"

Mgr: (After checking with the people), "That's 2 1/2 people."

And so on it went, item by item until the total was 5 people.

Pres: "That is enough! What do you have to do to make continuous improvements in the quality and productivity of payroll work?"

Mgr: "Find out the causes of all those troubles, errors, mistakes, complexities, queries, and get rid of them. Get rid of them in such a way that they don't return."

Pres: "That's right. I will tell the Treasurer of the major new project you are undertaking to do just that, and then I will go back to the V. P. Finance. I am going to ask him to join you as a joint project leader to help carry out the project and at the same time learn how to help all the rest of the financial and administrative managers."

The President spoke to both the Treasurer and V. P. of Finance. The V. P. agreed to take over joint project leadership. The following week, at the monthly general management meeting, the President made a brief announcement of the payroll project and the joint leadership. At the next few monthly general management meetings, the V. P. made five minute progress reports. After three months, the Payroll Manager and Vice President reported that productivity had already doubled. There were only 3 people now in the department. Service, timing, and accuracy were better than ever. They showed data and facts to prove it. One person retired and two were transferred to work in other areas of the company. Many of the troubles were gone.

Even more important than the yearly savings of $100,000 to $150,000 was the change of behavior in the Vice President of Finance. He had thought his area was working on quality improvement, but he had really been focusing on peripheral projects—mostly small incremental projects. After this experience, the Vice President of Finance knew what to do and how to do it. Within three to four months he had helped the Treasurer, Controller, and twelve department heads to work the new way. He had become a true leader of the change. Then the next level became leaders!

Early in the project to improve the quality and productivity of Payroll Department work, the team collected the following data over a three week period on how the hours were spent:

Hours Spent By Activity

Week	1	2	3	Total	Average
Data Entry	16	24	20	60	20
Work on Troubles	152	146	122	420	140
Incentive Pay	20	18	22	60	20
Special Queries	20	30	40	90	30
All Other	32	22	36	90	30
TOTAL	240	240	240	720	240

As an exercise in helping people to find the waste, ask yourself the following questions about this data:

- What is the problem?
- What is the project?
- What processes would you improve?
- What are the key performance measurements?
- How would you attack the problem?
- What sub-projects would you use?
- What tools or other help would you need?
- What was the most important thing the Vice President and Payroll Manager learned?

GET EVERYONE INVOLVED QUICKLY

A senior executive can skip the chain of command and work in the lower branches to help someone get started, provided everyone is open about it and accepts help. However, this approach is very time consuming, it may cause dissension in the ranks of intermediate management, and a senior executive of a large organization cannot afford the time to repair all the "breaks in the chain" of leadership. A much better approach is for the senior executive to involve people in the next level or two, so that they, too, become leaders of change.

Case: A Catalyst in Every Group
Another approach was used very effectively by Captain Bob McClendon, U.S. Navy, when he was commanding officer of the U.S. Navy Recruit Training Command, San Diego. In those days well before "Total Quality Management" or "Total Quality Leadership" had any meaning, Bob had heard of the principles of Drs. Shewhart, Deming, Juran and my work, and had read of the tremendous impact on some sectors of the business world. Bob believed that the recruit training staff of approximately 500 officers and enlisted personnel, and the annual student load of approxi-

mately 25,000 recruits offered a great opportunity to put the continuous improvement principles to work. Since the training cycle was eight weeks per recruit, the situation seemed well suited for data-based decision making, gathering and generation of improvement ideas.

Armed with some basic awareness and management tools education from a brief course provided by the Navy, Bob and some of his senior staff studied diligently to create an in-house plan for education and implementation. They were especially concerned about three major items: (1) The fear that was sure to arise from a "new" approach, (2) The approximately 30% turnover the staff would suffer each year, and (3) The very limited time Bob himself would be on board to lead the transition from the "old" to the "new" way.

All three of these concerns pointed to the difficult requirement to spread the required knowledge and attitude quickly throughout the organization. Bob decided to provide awareness and skills training to all upper management personnel, then allow a brief period to internalize what they had learned. Because he knew their past experiences and personalities would affect the speed with which the individual senior leaders could move into action, Bob did not issue quotas or threats. He did, however, tell the senior people that those junior to them would soon be given the same basic training and that the seniors should strive to understand the principles so they could help educate the juniors. He further emphasized that the "new" way would be process focused and that all people who participated in the improvements would be heard as "process experts" or "cross-functional team members" rather than just having the senior member assuming all the responsibility or the liability. Team leadership would be assigned or decided within the teams, depending upon a combination of expertise, experience, leadership skills, organizational credibility, or other needs of the organization. It would not necessarily fall to the senior person on the team.

Once the upper and middle management levels were trained,

they identified the primary processes of the organization, set priorities, and shared the information with the remainder of the organization. After the key processes were identified, the "worker-teams" who actually accomplished the work became apparent and natural leaders within those teams began to surface, regardless of age or paygrade. As those leaders emerged, they were encouraged to learn more and use their influence to make their work and their team even better. Meanwhile, their successes were shared throughout the organization to reward the leaders and to encourage others. Weekly organization-wide sessions were held to discuss achievements and concerns. Those one or two early leaders from each workgroup or team publicly shared their experiences and served as catalysts within the larger, more traditional workgroups. After approximately six months, there were thirty-seven of these peer-leaders in the "new way to work." Some of them had rank or seniority, others did not. They all had the desire to make their work measurably better and they had the support of senior leadership to do it! As those early leaders became more confident and educated in process improvement, they became more and more valuable as teachers and examples within the organization.

Various teams learned enough about how they worked and how to improve it to achieve very meaningful improvement projects! There were many tax-money saving projects that were achieved using simple tools and carried out by people interested in doing their work better. Throughout, this organization had strong upper leadership at the local level. Remember, at this point "Total Quality" was totally new outside the industrial activities of the Navy and most people at the operating level had never heard of it. There was clearly a perceived risk involved in trying it!

The approach worked like a charm! Rather than proceeding strictly level by level, each level of the chain of command was educated, then "process" focus allowed participation from any level that was ready to make supportable input. Leaders at several levels and in many different processes were identified early and became invaluable in helping others get started. Bob had people throughout the organization that he knew he could count on to help other people work in quality. Everyone knew what Bob was trying to do, even if they were reluctant to try or didn't understand it. He wasn't trying to hide anything. It wasn't secret. Peer leaders weren't being subversive. They just acted as catalysts to speed up changes and get continuous improvement started in their various areas of expertise. This case demonstrates another way of rapidly spreading continuous improvement. While total change is slow, it does not take 3 or 5 or 10 years to get started making very significant improvement!

OVERCOME RESISTANCE

One of the greatest sources of resistance to continuous improvement that a leader will encounter is the negativity of people who "know" that "it can't be done." In our photo finishing business, we had to ask some tough questions, get very specific data, and prove that it *could* be done in order to make the division profitable.

Case: Leveling Work and Staffing in Photo Finishing
By mid 1981, we had done enough serious work in some of our divisions to know that in any business we concentrated on, we could make dramatic improvements over a period of just a few years.

Our mail order photo finishing business had around $30 million in sales but was not making any money. It had been profitable for the first 8-10 years after we acquired two companies to enter the business. Then the market started a large and rapid shift. You might remember the Fotomat huts with overnight processing that sprang up everywhere in the late 70's. Also supermarkets started to use photo finishing as a bargain-priced promotional item to attract people to the store since it required two visits—to drop off the film and to pick up the prints.

These very substantial changes in the business eroded our profits over a period of a few years. We were running around break-even, lose a little money, make a little money. The salaried people and some hourly people had been to Dr. Deming's 4-day seminar. The managers and supervisors had projects, and people were trained on the simple statistical tools. They were, like most businesses in the United States today, doing a little work on quality, but thinking they were really covering all the bases. Now that we really knew what could be done, however, I realized that they weren't doing very much at all—just as most organizations in the United States today really aren't doing that much.

I decided to devote some of my time and energy to the business. I asked the Vice President and General Manager and a few senior people in the division to visit with me. We discussed what could be done in photo finishing to make it a profitable growth business by increasing sales, products, services, profits, return on assets and people. One thing they brought out right away was the importance of "people cost." A big part of the cost of photo finishing, much larger than at our other businesses, was people. The operations were filled with hand work. We promoted our services primarily by distributing mailing envelopes like the ones you see in the Sunday newspapers. When we received an order in the mail we opened the envelope, gave the order and the film(s) an identification number, and routed the work for processing. A single piece of mail could include a mixed order of film processing and/or reprints, enlargements, and slides in one envelope. We would do the processing work and then return the finished product and associated paperwork to the customer. The average value of an order at that time was about $5.25, which gives you an idea of the importance of effective work and work processes in this business. You had to promote the service, get the order in, do all the processing, price it according to the number of good prints, match the price with the money received, issue a charge or credit, and mail it back with the prints or slides. The normal cost just to enter orders in most businesses is around $50-100! In this case, the whole order was only worth $5.25. You had to have a very effective level of work to survive!

Quickly the conversation with the General Manager, the Manufacturing Manager and the other senior managers got around to the people costs. I said, "We have to make dramatic improvements—probably something like doubling the productivity, not a 5% or 10% improvement, if we are going to make the kind of change that we would like. What's the level of productivity now?"

None of them had a chart of productivity. A few days later they brought me a chart of productivity calculated by week. With all employees in all areas included in the calculation, they were averaging 12.3 orders per hour of work, varying from 10 to 14 with random variation. They felt there was not much they could do about it except to spend money for automation. Finally, they started to talk—maybe we could improve here or there.

Fortunately, I was involved in getting us into photo finishing, so I knew quite a bit about the business. I said, "I remember in the mail order business the big day for receiving mail is Monday. If customers mail it Friday, Saturday or Sunday we get it Monday or Tuesday morning, so we have a very heavy work load on Monday and part of Tuesday and then it slacks off during the rest of the week. Is that right? This chart by week doesn't mean anything to me. I'd like to see the chart the way it is on Monday, Tuesday, Wednesday—by day. If it is significant, we may want to see it by hour but most certainly by day."

At the end of the week I received the chart, and one look showed that on Monday productivity averaged about 21-22 orders per employee hour, varying from 18 to 25. The rest of the week it averaged just a little over 10, giving a weekly average of 12.3. I looked at it and said (with all the senior 5 or 6 managers of the business there), "Well, that's very straightforward."

They said, "What do you mean?"

I said, "I want every day to be Monday. Every day Monday. Let's get going. We must get every day to be Monday over the next nine months. Every day is a Monday."

Right away, they listed all the reasons we couldn't do it. We guaranteed our customers 24-hour turnaround—everything that we received had to be processed and shipped within 24 hours. We needed to have the people available for surges in business. We had all these permanent employees. On and on it went. In order to get them started, I gave several suggestions—hire part-time help who work only one or two days a week, save reprint and enlargement work for later in the week, find some outside work without deadlines that you can do on a subcontract basis. I said, "I don't need to go through all the possibilities. You people go through that and figure out how we are going to do it."

They responded, "We can't possibly get people to work on just Monday and Tuesday." They had every reason why things wouldn't work.

I said, "Don't tell me all the reasons it won't work. Find out the reasons that it will work and let's make it work. Let's go, team!"

As soon as they found all the reasons why the work wasn't level and what they could do about it, they were able to solve the problem effectively. We had another small photo finishing plant two hundred miles away that was totally uneconomic and had to be closed. When that plant was closed all that mail order business was moved into the main plant in Parkersburg, West Virginia.

With the added volume we didn't add any permanent staff. We found a number of people who didn't want full-time work and were happy to work part-time Monday and/or Tuesday. In fact we achieved such flexibility that we could weigh the mail first thing Monday morning, compute from that how many workers we would need, and call in the proper number of part-timers. We made many other improvements. We built up our volume and ten months to a year later, we had every day a Monday! We brought the average up from 12.3 to 20 orders per employee by finding out all the reasons why every day was not a Monday and then making Mondays.

That didn't mean we were finished. We'd almost doubled the productivity. We had made big improvements in quality for the customer, yet now we could all see that we had barely started. There were huge improvements still to be made in the photo finishing business. So much starts with the determination to learn all about the work. Once we understand the work, we find the waste and can make the big improvements.

This story illustrates an important principle. One of the biggest causes of waste is the mismatch between work to be done and the number of people to accomplish it. Parkinson's First Law states that "Work expands to fill the time available." In other words if people don't have sufficient value-added work to do, people will find something else to fill the hours. It is up to management to provide full-time, meaningful work for all employees. That's what people want ! This may require leveling the work, having a flexible work force, increasing volume, getting different kinds of work, making improvements to drive down cycle time, or arranging a combination of some of these efforts. An effective leader won't accept "we can't do it" as a response and will ask questions that lead to finding the waste caused by factors such as an uneven supply of work.

The managers of that division were now fully motivated believers. Over the next four years, they worked the new way in all areas, taking advantage of changes in information technology. As a result of the new ideas from marketing and sales, the rate of return of promotional envelopes more than doubled. The company grew, created jobs, hired more people, and became #1 in the American and British markets. Nowadays people call such major innovations "reengineering." We reengineered the entire business into being WORLD CLASS.

RECOGNIZE THE VITAL FEW

One of the most important jobs of a leader is to help people work on the right things. Continuous improvement takes concentrated effort. You cannot work effectively on everything at once. The leader of each organization and of each part of the organization, along with his or her team, must identify those "vital few" projects that can make a real difference.

Several criteria apply to picking these major projects:

- The potential for improvement (elimination of waste) should be substantial; continuous improvement includes all major changes as well as incremental changes.
- The leadership and process operators in the area chosen should believe in continuous improvement.
- The management should be ready to provide the leadership, drive, resources, innovation and creativity to carry out the project.
- The project should be in an area of significance to the organization's success.

Identifying and quantifying the waste is the beginning point in choosing projects. Look for the big opportunities to cut costs, improve quality, reduce time or increase revenues that can be accomplished relatively easily. Choosing what to work on is the most important decision anyone makes.

Case: Refocusing the Exploration Division

Work with an American oil company illustrates the importance of focusing on the right things, and how difficult it is, sometimes, for people within the business to see what those few vital things are. Asking the right questions sometimes will help them.

We had done some seminars for various departments of a major oil company, including one for the Exploration and Production Department. Many people showed interest and yet, at the next meeting, I would find that very few people were really finding the waste and getting rid of it permanently. Here and there people would make incremental improvements, but really they were small projects. They never seemed to get at the fundamentals of the business for substantial improvement. Clearly, the work was not being driven by top and senior management. People talked about customers and human relations. Everyone cooperated, people had charts, and they had team training. They thought they were all set and we explained to them that they were going to need more help. They said they didn't need any consulting help, they didn't need any more workshops, they were all set. They were on their own.

About a year and a half later, the top people called to say they would like to meet with me. For the first 30 minutes of our meeting they told me what they were doing in continuous improvement. I made notes of the main points that they said and listed the things they were doing and trying to carry out. When they were finished, I asked certain questions. What are you really trying to do? What is the market? What are the outside world and the market telling you that you must do? What should you really be trying to accomplish? Why are you doing what you are doing? What is your mission, your vision?

They had their piece of paper with the mission and vision. It was "boiler-plate" material. When they got away from the written mission and I asked them questions, their answers were all over the place. I asked more questions leading to what it was they were really trying to do. What would make their department and thereby the whole organization the greatest oil company in the world? What would be the quantum leap that would put them out in front of everyone? After about 20 or 30 minutes of discussion two of us summarized the key points.

"Find lots of oil at low cost, not only low exploration cost, but also low production and transportation and refining cost, in places where the oil is easy to get out—physically, environmentally and politically." Everyone agreed that was what they wanted to do. I said, "Let's go back to our discussion at the start of the meeting and go over the things that you told me you are doing." I got out my notes and read them aloud. I said, "What's that got to do with finding oil that is low cost from every standpoint, oil in places easy to get out, physically, environmentally and politically?" They agreed that practically everything had little to do with vital objectives. I said, "You see, you are not working on the *Vital Few*. You are working on the wrong things." In this case the internal customer was the rest of the oil company, and the external customers were the distributors, dealers and consumers. Many things they were working on did not add value from the external customer's viewpoint.

Working on day-to-day problems often keeps us from seeing the vital few things that will make the big difference in the success of an organization. A good leader will work to identify the fundamental tasks and gain the consensus of the rest of the organization to concentrate their efforts on these vital few. A clear, simple mission statement that everyone agrees to is a key item no matter what business a company is in. Working from such a statement will lead to the vital few. Too many people work on the urgent rather than the important. Then we focus the energy of our best people to change the major processes to make the leap to the best in the world. We used to call these projects "Major Management Directed Programs."

FOCUS ON WASTE

Focusing on finding the waste is a powerful tool in organizing improvement efforts. Soon people understand that there is a lot of waste and that you are focusing on how to eliminate it, rather than on placing blame. Then they can concentrate on the achievements possible in finding and eliminating the waste. They will not feel guilty or worried that they have allowed the waste to accumulate, since you have accepted that accumulation as a natural consequence of the old system of management. Nobody should have anything to hide. Amnesty is given for past mistakes.

Continuous improvement is critical, but for most people the phrase is too vague, other than as a rallying cry. Most organizations do not really understand continuous improvement and far too many people believe there is almost no waste. They think it refers mainly to improvements made at low and middle levels of the organization. Continuous improvement includes such changes, but the most important changes are those fundamental and major changes that only top management can lead. Finding, quantifying, and eliminating waste—including waste of lost sales and lost opportunity, growing the business and creating jobs—that leads to continuous improvement, and it is a specific focus that everyone can understand. Often people cannot see the waste because they are too close to it. People need leadership to help them see the waste. The leader needs education and training to ask the right questions to discover the waste. Other people do too. A number of cases in this chapter demonstrate how leaders moved people into action to find and eliminate the waste.

Case: Leading the Attack on Waste at Dow

If you have a very large organization and want to get started quickly, you need some way to move a lot of people into action. Larry Wright showed just how much difference a good leader could make when he went after the waste in the Texas Division of Dow Chemical. Larry, who had recently been promoted to Vice President and General Manager for Dow Texas, had heard me make 4 hour presentations on The Right Way To Manage, twice at the Michigan Division of Dow USA, and he was vitally interested in starting to work in quality. He was a firm believer.

I went to Dow Texas along with three others from our firm to run a two-day seminar for the top 85 people from all areas of the company, including Finance, R&D, Engineering, Maintenance and Manufacturing. In his opening remarks to the group, Larry said that he hoped everyone would pay close attention to the seminar. He had heard the message before in Midland, Michigan, and wanted everyone to know that this was the way everyone was going to work at Dow Texas. He hoped they would pay very careful attention because when they went to work on Wednesday morning he expected that they would start working the New Way.

Larry sat in the first or second row during the entire seminar. Anytime there was any shortage of questions or comments, Larry or a member of the Operating Board would ask a couple of questions to keep the interest high. But it was Larry's closing comments that really got people moving.

He said, "Ladies and gentlemen, I want you to know that while we have been at the meeting, my secretary has been working. She has been calling responsible people in each of the organizations, making appointments with you on your calendar to meet with me for about half an hour to an hour sometime in the next few days. I expect you to tell me two things. One, the personal things that you are going to do right now in accordance with thinking the New Way about waste and quality. What actions are you taking to get rid of waste? What is it that you are going to do yourself to show evidence of your belief and willingness to work in the New Way? In addition, you will tell me of a project you will start, working with people in your organization. It will utilize the tools that Bill has talked about to get rid of the waste by improving the process, to find the fundamental troubles and problems, to get rid of them, and to prevent their return."

"You will be working together as a team with a group of people to accomplish a common goal. I want something that is substantially within your own control, that you can complete within 90 days, and that you will be able to measure. I am also arranging another meeting with you 90 days from now. At that meeting you are going to tell me what you did, what you accomplished, and you are going to bring evidence--the data and the charts--to show what you and the project team have done to make these improvements."

He and his Operating Board recognized that he needed to move people into action. The power of Larry's position allowed him to do it. He didn't wait for motivation. He had enough faith in the system to know that the successes to come would provide the motivation.

We ran a great number of one- or two-day seminars at Dow Texas. For several years, many of Larry Wright's people continued to come to our 3-day public seminars in New Hampshire. Every time I have been to Dow Texas, Larry Wright was available to open the seminar and sometimes to close the seminar as well. He makes remarks similar to those he made on the first day. When Larry was asked what he would do differently, if he were doing it again, he says, "I would do a lot more heavy education and training of everyone in a much shorter period of time in order to move them into action faster in working the New Way."

Larry announced in his public speech to the NASA First Annual Quality Conference that the prior year improvements had a value of $44 million per year. In the following year *Dow Today*, an internal but public document, reported improvements of $100 million. Larry and his team moved from incremental improvements to major changes. Larry Wright is one of the true leaders of real continuous improvement through quality in the United States, and he is doing it at a very senior level. In 1990 he was promoted to be Vice President of Operations, Dow USA.

FIND WASTE FROM LOST SALES OR OPPORTUNITIES

Often the biggest waste is not in costs or expenses but in failing to take advantage of opportunities to increase sales from new products, new marketing programs, increases in capacity from the elimination of bottlenecks, quality improvements, cost reductions, etc. - all to make a successful growth business.

Case: Increasing Oil Well Productivity

My work with a leading foreign petroleum company underscored the point that increasing overall production may not be as important as increasing production of a key product. Asking the right questions uncovered the opportunity and provided the impetus to action.

In early Spring, the Vice President of Production attended our three day public seminar in Nashua. Sitting next to him at dinner, after the first day of the seminar, I asked him what he did. He told me he was the Vice President of Production and I asked him what that meant.

He said, "I am responsible for the digging, drilling of the hole, and getting the pipes in the ground and getting the oil up through the pipe and through a collection system with pumps and sumps until we get it into the big pipe, headed on the way to the refinery." Including independent contractors, he had 10,000 people working with him.

We talked about some of the problems that they had in maintaining the pumps and pipes. We also discussed some of the things that go wrong in the wells. He told me that because his company had many wells 20-50 miles away, spread out over a wide area, people were paid for all their time in travel. This arrangement wastes money as well as time. Sometimes they fly out in helicopters to save time.

Although I didn't discourage him from looking for ways to reduce this obvious source of waste, I said, "There is often a big source of waste that people do not see—the waste of product or service not sold. Many times the easiest place to find waste in big quantities is where sales are restrained by capacity for some product. Often by removing that restraint you can make the organization much more profitable over both the short and long run. If you had more of this oil could you sell it?" I was looking for the "blue whales" not just the minnows and the mackerel.

It turned out that outside restraints limited their sales of some kinds of oil but that there was always a market for a special light crude that came from their off-shore wells. We talked about what the potential for more oil might be and I said, "Are all the oil wells optimized?"

"What do you mean, optimized? I believe we are getting out all the oil we can."

"But are you getting the oil out of the ground as fast as you could and should if everything were perfect with the well?"

"Oh, I doubt it. You know, we set the well up, we drill it, and it runs on. If it really goes bad we go back there and do some more work on the well. No, I suppose they're not really optimized."

"How many wells do you have?"

"Thousands."

"Who optimizes these wells?"

"The Petroleum Engineer."

"How many Petroleum Engineers do you have?"

"Over 100."

I said, "What we could do is this. I'm not a statistician but I'll make a rough estimate. Select 25 of those wells at random. Then have the best Petroleum Engineers, using the best known processes, optimize each of those 25 wells. You will know what the history of the well is, what it has been producing before, and now you are going to see the data, the change—how much that increases as well as the cost and time to do it. Follow that data to see how fast it comes back down. Clearly, if it takes three days to optimize a well and in one day it is back to where it was, then of course there's no sense in doing it.

"Optimizing an oil well is like keeping a machine tool sharp. At first the machine tool is very sharp and is cutting the right dimension in the part, but gradually it wears. That's what is happening here. Something is wearing or getting out of adjustment in the oil well that is tending to make it produce less than the optimum."

I asked how the wells were optimized and he described one major device. A separate pipe goes down into the well to carry natural gas that can be injected at high pressure at various levels. They use the injection of that gas to pressurize the reservoir to optimize the rate at which the oil is forced up the pipe. He also said there were numerous other ways to improve the flow from the well.

I said, "Let's prioritize the wells, inject natural gas and work on the other major factors affecting their production. We are going to optimize the important factors so we optimize the system and see what happens." The company put its best people in charge of the project and on the project team. They had the resources they needed and the power and authority to make it happen.

In the discussion at that time, several experienced oil people estimated they could get an additional 50,000 to 100,000 barrels of oil per day. Since they had a cap on total production, the estimated gain was only on the premium price for the light crude or an extra $2.50 per barrel. At 100,000 barrels/day, the gain would amount to $250,000 per day or $90,000,000 per year.

When I visited five months later they were already well into optimizing the wells, using 50 Petroleum Engineers. The volume was already up but was still bouncing around with good days and bad days, so they weren't quite ready to say what they had achieved. By that fall, production was already up some 30,000 to 40,000 barrels a day. The next time I asked, it was up 65,000 to 70,000 barrels a day. Within 2 years it was up over 100,000 barrels a day and continuing to move higher.

By early 1990 the premium on that oil was a minimum of $4.50 a barrel. 100,000 barrels at $4.50 a barrel is $450,000 per day. That means an additional $165 million a year. During the Iraq-U.N. war, when Iraq was not producing oil and everyone lifted production caps, sweet crude was selling for $27 per barrel. Subtracting a marginal cost of $5 per barrel leaves a profit of $22 per barrel because all the oil produced was now in excess of previous total production. 100,000 barrels per day x $15 per barrel x 350 days per year equals approximately $525 million per year. Since the area had oil in the ground for the next century this was not a case of just using up a near-term asset.

Even though this project did not concentrate on reducing costs and expense, or on customer satisfaction, it was probably the most meaningful project in the company in its effect on profits. This led to real enthusiasm for working the new way. It is important to look at the fundamentals of the business and try to discover those few things that, if improved, would have a major effect. In this case, capitalizing on a hidden opportunity paid off handsomely. It was another major process change that included much innovation and creativity by the project team.

APPLY THE NEW APPROACH TO EVERY FUNCTION

Often people assume that finding the waste applies only to manufacturing activities. Discovering the waste in sales and administrative activities is more difficult, and it is hardest of all in the professional and staff areas, such as research and development or the legal department. People are generally working hard and do not think there is any waste. But with the right tools, questions, and attitudes, we can find it.

Case: What about the Legal Staff?

I was asked to visit with the President and COO of a major consumer products company, along with the 18 top people from all over the world. I had been working with their central Research and Development group and the Director of that R&D group had described to the President what Conway Quality had been doing for them. We had identified the vital few things to improve. We had studied the work, using work sampling and other techniques, and found huge opportunities to eliminate waste and improve the work.

My job was to make an hour and a half presentation, starting at 10 o'clock, followed by half an hour of questions and answers. The questions and answers were still going on at 2 o'clock. No one had any lunch. Shortly after 2:00 the President interrupted and said, "Mr. Conway, that gentleman on my left in the middle seat is the general counsel of the corporation. We have many lawyers working for us. We have many consumer products and the associated problems. We have lawsuits on everything: R&D, patents, OSHA, and everything you can imagine. We have both inside lawyers and ones we hire from outside. Our chief counsel came to me a month ago and said that I was always talking about quality. He was listening to me but he did not know what to do for quality and he wondered if I could tell him. Mr. Conway, I did not know what to tell him. What should I have told him?"

I knew then I was having my final examination. If I could not tell the President how to help lawyers then the chances were small that we would do any more business with this large company.

I asked for a couple of minutes to think it over before I gave my answer. I knew that I would have to show them how to find the waste and move into action in the legal department.

I made a mental list of the principles and techniques that applied:

- Identify and survey the customers
- Identify the work that adds value
- Insure people are working on the right things and are working effectively
- Gather data
- Provide needed education and training
- Use work sampling to help identify the work that adds value and help insure that people are working on the right things.
- Try to make sure the suppliers are also working the new way
- Move people into action

Then I started to share my thoughts. "Start here in the United States where you have over 60,000 employees. Identify the major customers of the corporate legal department in the United States. They would probably be the general managers of your various businesses, with questions about the way they market, questions in regard to various anti-trust laws, the Robinson-Patman Act, etc. Your customers would also be the central R&D people who wonder about things like patents and technical agreements with other firms. Facilities, Maintenance and Human Resources people would have questions on OSHA. Sales and Marketing people worry about pricing and what they can say to customers about competitors.

"I imagine you would come up with a list of 1,000 - 1,500 people that would be major customers of the corporate legal department. Survey those customers to find out what to work on. What should the legal department work on to maximize the long run benefits from legal services for the corporation? Collect the data on what you work on now, and compare that with what the customers thought the priority for those things should be. In this case your 'internal customers' would tell you what you should be doing.

"Next look at all the requests for legal work. What are all the things on which people come to you to ask for help? Get data for the last 90 days. Now, study that list of the requests for legal services. Categorize those requests as ones that people should come to you to ask and ones that should not have to come to you. Many times when people come to you for legal services, they are really just covering themselves because they do not want to be blamed if something goes wrong. They really should not ask, but they do. On a great many items people should have been educated and trained so they knew what to do without asking. If you had educated and trained the people, they would know when they should ask and when they should not. You would provide them a clearly defined set of rules distinguishing the things on which they should make their own decisions from the questions that really do require legal help.

"The next thing I would determine is all the waste that the legal department causes all the rest of the people. For this you would survey a much larger group working for the company in the United States, probably 7,000 - 8,000 people, including people that fill out forms and provide information for the SEC, OSHA or other government agencies. Find out what waste you cause all the people. You may send forms to more than one person when you do not need to. Maybe you should send them the information from the previous years so they can see how questions have been answered in the past and can fill out the form in much less time than it now takes.

"Could you use a central computer file from which you could easily retrieve information so that people did not have to process forms again? All that type of thing. I would gather data on all the waste the legal department causes other people--not just in filling out forms, but in any work, any investigations they were involved in for the legal department.

"Next I would ask all the legal people what they thought they should be working on to be of the most benefit to the organization. Why? and How?

"At the same time this was going on, people in the legal department and outside lawyers working for you would sample their own work. What are they doing for work? For what periods of time? What you find from the survey of your customers is probably what you should be working on. You would see what you have been working on; you would see what the incoming requests are. You would set in motion a series of projects for improvement so you would stop things coming in on which you should not work. You would work on the right things. You would select major legal work processes for improvement, study the processes, and make continuous improvements. You would reorient the work of the legal department and outside attorneys to get all the work in line with those things to benefit the overall business.

"At the same time find out what your present work is. You'd find there is available time to carry out the added work because you are full of waste. Start projects to improve the work that remains. This whole process is an ongoing one. The big change would come in the first two years as you got rid of work you should not do, worked on the right thing, and then improved the work you should do. You would repeat your surveys at appropriate intervals to make certain you continued to work on the right things."

When I finished after seven minutes, the President thought for a couple of minutes, then smashed his hands on the table. He said,

"Ladies and gentlemen, we have heard Bill for over four hours. We have thought that we have been working in quality for the last few years. We have done some good things on the repetitive work and the continuous processes in the plant. As far as getting everyone in the company to work the New Way, as far as really working on the major processes for huge changes—doubling, tripling, quality and productivity, major cost reduction through supplier partnerships and engineering design process, major changes in policies and procedures, etc.—we have not done it at all. Bill asked us this question before: how many people do we have in the whole company that actually make things? We have well over 100,000 employees. I checked and less than 20% actually make things. We have over 100,000 people that we are hardly touching in real continuous improvement through quality. No wonder we have a hard time competing. We should work on some big things as well as small. We need breakthroughs. We are going to start this afternoon towards working the New Way Bill talked about."

Within thirty days they had concluded that they had far too many people. They stopped hiring, they started making improvements, and over the next year they improved productivity by over 10%. With facts and data, they now saw current reality in a new light. They even started real improvements in the legal department.

This example shows that the organized search for waste and continuous improvement can apply to any type of work. If it applies to lawyers, it can apply to everyone and everything! Since nearly 85% of American workers work outside the manufacturing sector, it is important to learn how to find the waste and eliminate it in all areas of work. The four guiding principles are: 1) Focus on finding, quantifying and eliminating the waste, 2) Move people into action in the right direction, 3) Having determined the big wastes, go to work to change and improve the major processes that cause the waste and get rid of it and 4) Treat people as we would like to be treated. All the other principles and tools support these four fundamentals.

All of these examples show various ways these four principles can be implemented. Every organization is different and each requires a somewhat different approach, but by following these four fundamental guides a leader can get big things started as well as encourage numerous process improvements to eliminate the smaller and more local wastes.

FIND THE WASTE WHERE "THERE ISN'T ANY"

Sometimes waste is easy to find, and reducing it just requires careful analysis and imaginative solutions. But often everyone "knows" that there's no waste in a particular area because the organization seems to have no control over certain costs and expenses. Overcoming such resistance requires determined leadership and imagineering at all levels.

Case: More Photo Finishing Waste

In the mail-order photo finishing business at Nashua Corporation, we had made great progress in improving profitability by leveling the work. But I knew that we still needed to identify and quantify other waste throughout the division. We had sales of about $30,000,000 but still weren't making much money. Sales were expanding and the division manager requested a budget of $1,100,000 for new machinery and equipment.

I said that before we approved any such request, we had to identify and quantify the waste in the business. To get at it, I asked for a breakdown of where all the money went. We wanted to find the four, five or six things which consumed the most money and start attacking the waste in each one. We came up with the following list of major costs and expenses.

Salaries and wages	$ 7,100,000
Advertising and sales promotion	$ 5,900,000
Postage	$ 4,900,000
Photographic paper for color prints	$ 4,700,000

These four items consumed more than three quarters of our sales revenues.

We established teams to identify, quantify and eliminate the waste in each area. The teams came back with their estimates of waste.

Salaries and wages	19 %
Advertising and sales promotion	1 %
Postage	0.5 %
Photographic paper for color prints	1 %

I went over the estimates in detail with the team managers. After all the explanations, I said, "You've made a good start in the area of salaries and wages. With a lot of hard work, more work sampling and analysis of the work process, I think we can do better, but let's get started. Let's assign a couple of industrial engineers for three months to help with the methods improvements. Let's pick the major processes to make giant changes.

"As for the other three areas, I don't think you've even scratched the surface. We need to open our minds, imagineer and come up with some whole new approaches to cut the waste we don't even see."

There were lots of protests that we had already done everything we could. We were using the most cost-effective sales promotions, we had negotiated the best possible price for color print paper, and certainly we couldn't negotiate a lower rate with the Post Office. I said I wanted a whole new approach in each area. I didn't know what it was, or whether it would work, but I wanted them to come up with an idea that might make a significant difference in the cost of promotion, of postage, and of color print paper.

Today people would say we used reengineering. We called it a major management directed program using innovation and creativity and knowledge of work to make breakthroughs. The team studied the processes and came up with lots of ideas for improvement.

We were buying our color print paper from a Japanese supplier in 3½", 5", and 8" rolls. The supplier coated large master rolls of the paper, slit and cut it into small rolls and stocked the material in a refrigerated warehouse in the United States for its U.S. customers. Since we had experience in handling and slitting large rolls of paper (although not in total darkness) we proposed to the supplier that we stock the paper in master rolls and slit it as needed. As an added inducement to work this way, we said we would slit special orders for other customers. Since this saved them considerable freight and handling, they agreed to a large price reduction. They also agreed that we could pay for the paper 60 days after we slit it for our own use. This improved our cash flow and significantly reduced one of our major costs. We were now partners with the supplier—a real supplier partnership. We worked together.

Postage seemed more difficult. We made some minor changes to reduce the weight of the customer's package, but without much saving. We tried third class mail instead of first class, but when we had a customer far from our plant the service time deteriorated. Finally we worked with the post office and found that we could mail first class bulk express overnight to a postal sectional center and then send the individual orders third class from there. The average service time improved and our postage costs dropped by almost 30%—a truly incredible change from a significant innovation. We changed the mail system in a major way! Even after we knew the system would work it took 9 months of hard work to get it fully in place.

Most of the money we spent on marketing was for printing and distributing promotional envelopes. We would offer a low price and hope the customer would subsequently order at our regular price. Using coded envelopes, we continually tested to see which offers and distribution channels gave the best results. The ideal offer would be one that would yield "POFTO" (profit on first time order). If we could make sufficient margin on the first order to cover our marketing expense and still make a profit, we could expand the business indefinitely. The more we spent on getting

"POFTO" customers, the more money we made. Unfortunately, very few of our promotions yielded profits on our first order. Also our customers would continue looking for low priced promotional envelopes, and there was little customer loyalty.

Our major competitor's prices were lower than ours, and we had never felt we could make money at those prices. But since we were making progress in cost reductions, we decided to test considerably lower prices. The business came pouring in, reducing our promotional costs per order considerably. We then decided to try increasing customer loyalty by charging the same low price for repeat orders as our promotional price. Repeat orders increased dramatically, further lowering our marketing costs to get an order.

With the other improvements we were making, we found that we were making good margins at the lower prices, and our business began to expand rapidly. Nashua is now the world's largest mail order photo finishing company, the market leader in the United States, Canada and the United Kingdom. It operates on a very profitable basis. You may have seen its promotions under the name of York Photo in the United States.

This turnaround of the business and its development into a world-class operation was due to identifying the major cost elements, finding and eliminating the waste. The low costs gave the opportunity to lower the price and increase sales greatly. By finding the waste first, we could clearly identify the key processes to improve. As we changed and improved we measured both process and results. Creativity and innovation were everywhere. People felt great satisfaction. Even with tremendous productivity improvements employment increased with the volume changes. We made a real growth business, created more jobs, made more money. We took care of the employment security for everyone by eliminating the waste! It also required the willingness to have an open mind about what could be accomplished and the determination to find a new and better way of doing things.

SPEED UP THE CHANGES

Focusing on waste and moving people into action in the right direction are the keys. But often people move into action too slowly, and that very slowness creates narrow thinking about what can be accomplished. Sometimes it is helpful to create an artificial emergency to open people's minds. You can ask people what they would do if it were a national emergency, or if they were going out of business without urgent action. This keeps people from concentrating on reasons why it can't be done and opens their minds to new approaches. Another example illustrates how this method can be used.

Case: It's The Pump!

I visited a $1 billion division of a large chemical company. At that time prices were very depressed in the commodity chemical business and business was extremely difficult. I had been to this division before and knew the General Manager, Tom. At the end of the day, around 4:30, I'd often end up meeting with Tom in his office.

In the course of the discussion I asked how the business was going. He said they were still losing quite a bit of money, around $40 million a year, pre-tax, on their sales of about $1 billion.

Tom said, "I'd like to really get some projects going and get at some of the waste right now!"

I said, "Well, the biggest waste of all is almost always in the sales not made that should have been made, and the easiest ones to get are those not made due to so-called capacity. Tell me, do you have any important items in your product line that are running at so-called capacity?"

Tom named one that had sales of about $100 million a year. He added, "Yes, we run to capacity, all we can get out."

"What kind of gross margin and contribution to fixed expense do you have for that product?"

"I'd have to check further, Bill, but it's in the range of 25-30%."

"25-30%. Well, why don't we find out if we can sell more of it?"

"I'll be meeting the Commercial Manager, Vice President of all Commercial Activities, here about a week from now."

I said, "Why don't we find out now, Tom? Why don't we pick up the phone and call the people and find out now?"

"Now?"

"Yes, now. Just pick up the phone and find out."

So he did and a couple of minutes later he hung up and said, "Yes, they say they could sell at least 50% more. They're pretty confident as a matter of fact. They believe they can sell another $60 million and said they'd be able to get to that level within about 120 days. The Vice President of Sales confirmed, by the way, that the margin was around 30%, and asked that we let him know right away if there is anything he can do."

Tom added, "But I don't know what we can do about it, Bill. I had this big study made." He took an inch-thick engineering study out of his files. To expand 50% was going to take a year and a half and require $20 to 30 million.

He said, "With the terrible business conditions a year or so ago, we set it aside."

So I looked through it and said, "Well, I don't think we are going to need most of that, Tom, because the study talks about things to be done over the next few years and we only have about 90 days to do something big. There will, however, be some ideas there that will be very helpful to us. Let's get together the people that know something about the processes involved in making that product. Why don't we get the operators from that area of the plant, the people who run the equipment? And get the maintenance people, get the people that designed it, get the chemical engineers, the chemists that did some of the calculations and know most about the processes, get the plant superintendent who is running that area, and a couple of the other key people. Let's get together right now!"

"Bill, it's about a quarter to five. They all go home at 5 o'clock."

"Well, it would be a good time to get their attention. Why don't we get them all in here now?"

"You are serious, aren't you?"

"Yes, Tom, we ought to talk to them now, to make sure they all know that we are serious about trying to make continuous improvement."

His secretary made some calls and, shortly, the people started wandering in. Some were close by in their offices and some were out in the plant half a mile away. In the next 10 minutes most of the people had assembled. There were about 11 or 12 of them so we moved into a conference room and the General Manager introduced me and said, "Bill would like to discuss some of the ideas he has on how we can get more capacity for this chemical. I have already confirmed with the commercial people that we could sell a lot more if we could make it. You all know we are losing about $40 million pre-tax, but there's a chance here that we could get back a good portion of that just on this one product line."

I said, "Let's imagine we just got a call from the President of the United States. He told us that there was a new fungus that could destroy the U. S. grain crops. He said that this chemical for which we have limited capacity was the only thing they knew that could keep this fungus from spreading. As a matter of fact he said it would lead to food shortages throughout the world unless we were able to make very significant gains in production in the next 60 days. We need to increase 60%, another $60 million over our present $100 million in sales. Convert that into tons. We need to have production up in 60 days with equal or better quality. We are meeting here together to decide how we are going to do it. What are your ideas?

"What do we need? First, let me give you my definition of capacity. Capacity is a number put together by operating people, together with the financial people, based on a history of inadequate performance! That's what I visualize capacity to be! We are searching for our bottlenecks. What one thing, maybe two, could make a big difference in capacity? Maybe jump it 7, 8, 10, 15%. What are the first bottlenecks?"

Discussion started slowly. People had ideas. The person who had written that inch thick report of the one-to-two year program, with $20+ million of capital expenditures in it, spoke up. He said that he didn't see how we could possibly do anything—that a big study had been made that showed that major capital expenditures were required.

I thanked him very much and set the report aside. I told him that the report was interesting and perhaps he knew some ideas we could adopt that we could do within the next 60 days. I emphasized we had to do it within the next 60 days and that things a couple of years away are interesting but they wouldn't solve this problem. I suggested that he would be the best one to know which things we could do something about right away.

Ideas started to come. Over in the corner was a person who turned out to be a maintenance person in the area. He listened intently for a while and then said, "It's the pump, it's the pump."

But no one paid any attention.

A few more minutes went by and he said, "It's the pump, it's the pump," in a little louder voice.

I said, "Tell me, what is it you are talking about over there?"

He said, "It's the pump." And he named the type of pump. He added, "That pump is the key thing." He described how he knew that the pump was the bottleneck. He said, "It probably would be a gain of at least 10%, maybe as much as 15%. Just in that pump."

People started to discuss whether the pump was it and people said, "I think that he's right. It might well be the pump."

Then someone said, "To purchase a new pump costs over $1 million and delivery for the pump is around 9 months. We would never get the pump in 60 days."

The maintenance man said, "Well, I read all these magazines and it shows in the Used Equipment advertising that due to the closing of certain chemical plants some of these pumps are available. I think you can buy one of those pumps second hand. I think you can buy one and get delivery right away."

By now Tom was beginning to see that something could happen. He turned to the Director of Procurement, Purchasing. "Find out right now."

The maintenance man got the magazine and the suggested people to call. Five or ten minutes later, the Purchasing Director came back and said, "I've located a pump. We could get one in here in just a few days. And instead of $1 million, we can get it for $300,000—a second hand pump. It was in operating condition as late as six or eight weeks ago."

The General Manager said "Buy it! We can take care of the paperwork later, get it in here!"

One after another the ideas started to come. Plenty of ideas required further investigation, more details to justify, etc. They didn't do it in 60 days, but 90 days later they had their sales up another $60 million, with only a few million dollars in additional capital costs. The organization quickly cut its losses in half. We made a major change in the process by which improvements are made. We showed how everyone has lots of creativity and innovation. Leadership released it! We created the delta, the difference, the need for change.

What did we do? We showed that by creating an artificial sense of urgency we could release the power of the people, and tremendous things could happen very quickly.

LEAD WITH IMAGINEERING

Imagineering is one of the most powerful leadership tools for helping people to work in continuous improvement. My definition of imagineering is:

> The art of visualizing how things would be if everything were perfect, *no problems, no errors, no troubles of any kind.*

Or think of it as imagining a process with no waste, with everything done right. Imagineering has several advantages over conventional thinking.

- It immediately focuses attention on identifying waste. It looks for the difference, the variation, between the way things are now and the way they would be if everything were perfect. That difference represents waste, caused either by imperfect processes or by missed opportunities, including changes due to technology, capital investment, computers, marketing strategy, etc.
- It is a non-threatening, non-critical way of analyzing problems. Since people understand that nothing is perfect, they are not afraid to identify things that cause the process to be short of perfection.
- It gets people thinking about continuous improvement. Since perfection is a receding target, imagineering involves always moving toward perfection (continuous improvement) but never reaching it.
- It helps people think about big changes—reengineering or altering the entire system or process—as well as smaller improvements.
- It brings technology, capital investment, innovation and creativity to bear on significant problems and opportunities.
- It requires people to look at problems in a new way and brings forth ideas that otherwise wouldn't occur to people.
- It includes systems thinking and takes into account the time delays we often get in major systems and processes. People tend to think of change as instantaneous: one minute it's sunny, and the next minute it's pouring. But important changes often take a long time—it may take months of increased rains to fill the reservoir. Similarly, an organization may not see the effects of treating people better for two or three years. But imagineering can help us

see the effects of such changes, even though they're invisible initially in the quarterly profit report.

- It uses the brain power of the people involved in the process. They are the ones that can see the imperfections most clearly since they work with them every day. Asking people to identify ways that the process falls short of perfection often elicits better responses than just asking about troubles and problems. It can use the help of outsiders or outside experts. Everyone can contribute.
- It is an excellent tool for teams to use when working together to generate ideas.
- It helps to set priorities for improvement.
- It can be done at any level and with any boundaries. For instance, a group might want to imagineer only those solutions that a) use only current equipment and technology, or b) don't require capital investment, or c) require work only in a certain geographical area.

Imagineering requires hard work. To be effective, you usually need facts and knowledge. Group and/or individual imagineering sessions are greatly enhanced when you have the facts and data to fully understand the current situation. For a leader to be effective in encouraging imagineering, he or she must learn enough about a process to guide people in gathering the right data. After the data is gathered and converted to information, the leader should be willing to study it and participate in imagineering sessions.

Case: Imagineering in the Accounts Receivable Department

Consider how a leader who is concerned about reducing the time it takes to collect accounts receivable might proceed. Let's imagineer how this leader would use imagineering to attack the problem.

First, think about all the factors affecting accounts receivable and what groups and individuals are involved. Next, bring together a group representing all the areas that influence accounts receivable. This group would probably include someone from sales, marketing, manufacturing, warehousing, shipping, billing, data processing, credit and collections. Tell the group in advance that the purpose of the session will be to imagine and write down what the process would be like if everything were perfect, no errors, troubles or problems of any kind—nothing that would cause the customer to be dissatisfied and/or not pay an invoice on time. Ask the participants to bring any data that they already have, but not to gather any additional data at this point.

At the first meeting ask each participant to describe how things would be if everything were perfect in his or her area. Try to generate a free-flowing discussion where each builds on the other's ideas. People will think of specific past problems and will describe how the process would be without those problems. Write each comment on a board and summarize perfection at the end. The results might be:

- Salespeople always transmit the order accurately. They insure the customer understands what is being ordered. They obtain, and transmit accurately, any special shipping or billing instructions. Promise dates are consistent with manufacturing guidelines. Any exceptions to those guidelines are approved by manufacturing before the commitment is made.

- Manufacturing receives and schedules the order with sufficient leeway to insure meeting the scheduled ship date. Any increase in backlog is reflected in the guidelines given the salespeople. The product is produced according to the schedule and meets or exceeds customer requirements.

- The product(s) is properly identified and located so that when the order is complete, all of the components of the order are readily available. Any stock items that are to be added to the order are readily available. The order is accumulated for shipment on the promised shipment date. The order is correct, and there is no damage to any of the product. There are no back orders. The order is packaged properly and is loaded on the company truck or common carrier at the scheduled time. The carrier understands the delivery requirements and makes delivery on the promised date to the proper address with no damage to the product. The customer signs the proper receipts.

- Accurate and complete shipping documents which meet customer requirements accompany the shipment. At the same time, an invoice is prepared with an accurate and complete description of the shipment and with accurate pricing, including all the proper discounts. The date of shipment and expected delivery date are shown. The invoice is sent to the right address to the attention of the right customer employee. It arrives the same day as the shipment.

- The customer's accounts payable department matches the invoice with its receiving report and approves the invoice. Priority is given to paying the invoice within terms, since the customer considers you as a valuable and effective supplier. Also the accounts payable department has a good relationship with our billing department and wants to pay on time. The customer mails the complete payment to the proper address and it arrives promptly at the lock box or the accounts receivable department. It is deposited promptly in the company's account, and the customer is given the proper credit.

- We constantly add ideas such as eliminating the paper invoice using electronic data transfer and transferring the money electronically.

Most of the statements of perfection probably derived from some problem the company has had in the past. For example, several statements were made about promise dates and back orders, indicating that this may be a problem area. On the other hand, nothing was said about credit problems, an obvious area for most organizations. It may be that this particular company has very few credit problems. However, the leader of the meeting should question any obvious areas that have not been covered.

The next step is to determine what data should be gathered beyond what is already available. We need to know current reality. Where are we now? This data collection should be designed to help determine where there are real problems, how serious they are, and what priorities should be given to correcting them. A list of the data desired might be something like this:

- Number and per cent of orders during one month for which promised shipping dates were not within manufacturing guidelines.
- Number and percent of orders during one month that were not scheduled to meet promise date. Number and per cent that were scheduled properly, but nevertheless were late.
- Number and per cent of orders during one month that were incomplete on scheduled ship date, and a classification of the reasons.
- Number and per cent of orders during one month that were complete by scheduled ship date, but which did not reach customer on time, and a classification of the reasons.
- Number and per cent of errors in invoices during one month classified as to type of error.
- Analysis of customer complaints during one month classified as to type of complaint and reason.
- Survey of customers to find out the reasons they do not pay on time. This should not be done as a collection procedure, but the customer should be aware that this is part of a quality check to see what obstacles there are to reducing accounts receivable.
- Analysis of payment terms to determine if the present ones are the most effective.
- Process flow charts of all key work processes including times.

Assign people to gather this data giving them a reasonable amount of time to do it before the next imagineering meeting. At the next meeting review the data. On the basis of that review, the group should identify the most troublesome problem areas and establish priorities for further study. Smaller groups can meet to imagineer solutions to the problems discovered. Additional people with experience or expertise in these specific areas may be brought in as appropriate. These sub-group meetings solicit ideas as to how the process could be changed to make it run perfectly. More data may be needed. The groups should continue to break the problems down into smaller and smaller pieces until the solution to each piece becomes obvious.

At the same time, the larger group considers complete systems changes. How about making automatic transfers from a customer's account when the product is shipped or the service provided? The biggest gains usually come from such major changes which will then give the sub-groups new areas for work. Release the power of the people! Innovation! Creativity!

Imagineering Mind Set

The most powerful tool of continuous improvement is imagineering. We want everyone working in the organization to develop an imagineering mind set. Leaders in continuous improvement should think this way every hour of every day to set an example.

The previous section illustrated an organized way to imagineer the improvement of a process-major or minor. The leader in this exercise should point out how imagineering can be used by people in their everyday work in continuous improvement. By comparing what is being done presently with perfection, gathering data to see what causes the differences from perfection, and imagining ways to achieve it, people develop a mind set for continuous improvement.

Imagineering should become a way of thinking and communicating for the whole organization. When people accept the search for perfection as a way of life, it permeates their thinking about everyday problems and activities.   It becomes a powerful tool for improvement. Encourage people to think this way by continually using the approach in meetings and in one-on-one discussions. The leader should set the example and then encourage others to make imagineering a part of their daily work.

We know we have not reached and never will reach perfection. But we can use our image of perfection to identify and focus on areas where the process(es) falls short. We need to apply such imagineering to all areas of thinking about the organization and what it does. We can imagineer what business(es) we are in, how we design systems to conduct that business, what major processes we use, what sub-processes and sub-sub processes, etc. should make up the major processes. We can also imagineer the culture of the company and the way we work every day.

We can then gather data, analyze the differences from perfection, set priorities, and break the problems down into smaller and smaller pieces until needed changes become obvious. We make those needed changes, one by one, and move closer to perfection. As we make progress and learn more, we redefine perfection and review our priorities. This cycle of definition, analysis, improvement and redefinition will become a part of our everyday thinking. It will apply to thinking about the overall business strategy, major systems and major processes, and throughout the organization to the sub-processes and to individual work situations.

Imagineering Questions

Questions and the way they are asked help leaders inject imagineering for continuous improvement into people's thinking. Some generic questions are:

- Do we know why this process is important? What do our customers want? Is this the best way to serve our customers?

- Do we have a written description of what this process would be like if everything were perfect? What is the description of the current process?
- Do we have continuing input about the troubles and problems from the people working in the process?
- Do we imagineer at different levels as appropriate?
- What is the biggest roadblock to reaching perfection in this process?
- Do we have the data to see how far we are from perfection?
- What are the major things we need to do (to investigate) (to improve) to bring this work process much closer to perfection?
- Do we still have the big picture so we are trying completely new ways to do things?
- Have we divided the problem into small enough pieces so that the solution to each piece becomes obvious?
- Are the people working in the process encouraged to use imagineering on an everyday basis? To communicate their ideas? To make improvements on their own when they see an opportunity? To help their peers to make improvements? To feel "ownership" of, and responsibility for, their work process?

By continually showing interest and communicating about imagineering, a leader will encourage imagineering activities. Of course, most importantly the leader must use imagineering him/herself to encourage use by others. Imagineering works on the "big picture" or the "small picture", high tech or low tech, product design, administrative processes, new product development process, collecting receivables, anything! Imagineering is of major help in "growing the business." Our people want to see the organization creating opportunities for people as well as improving return on investment and profitability.

CHAPTER 2
EDUCATE AND ACT

EDUCATION AND TRAINING

People need education to see how and why the new system of working will benefit the organization and how it will benefit them personally. Education is different from training. Education teaches people what the management system of continuous improvement is all about and the reasoning behind it. Training provides the specific tools to be used in continuous improvement. Appendix C provides a detailed education and training program.

Education helps persuade people to participate and to support the required changes by showing people the benefits of the changes in terms of increased responsibility, achievement, and self-respect on the job. It demonstrates that this system can vastly improve the competitiveness of the organization. Companies often adopt this system because they are striving for excellence (aspiration), or struggling to be competitive (desperation). In either case people should understand the reasons for the changes in how people work and what outcome to expect.

Training, as opposed to education, should be designed to teach people specifically what needs to be done to change to the new system. It includes learning how to use the tools of continuous improvement, how to apply the principles of work, key concepts of variation, and how to work best with others.

All the people that are involved in the change should receive some education during a relatively short time period—three months to one year depending on the size of the organization. This gives everyone a feeling of participation and generates acceptance and the desire to move into action. Training, on the other hand, is most effective when it is done "just-in-time," that is, just before people will use it in a project. The effectiveness of the training diminishes rapidly if the tools are not used in practice. Make courses flexible—adapt them to the needs of the moment. Assure that the infrastructure for education and training is in place and the necessary resources are available.

THE CORE ACTIVITY

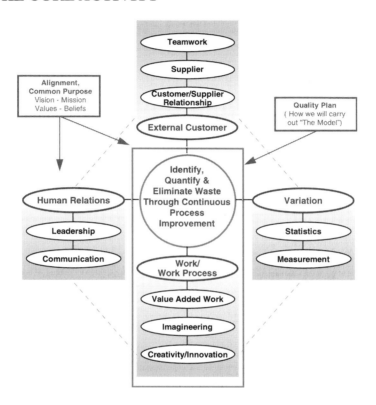

This diagram of the continuous improvement system shows that the central activity of the system is to "identify, quantify, and eliminate the waste through continuous process improvement."

To be truly effective this activity must be led by top and senior managers. Support comes from:

- Properly handling human relations
- Understanding and meeting customer needs
- Using the tools of variation; and, most importantly,
- Studying the work and work processes.

Focusing on the core activity of attacking waste is key to a successful system of continuous improvement. Reducing the waste in a process increases quality and productivity. Depending on competition, it usually improves profitability. Quality improves as the level of operations is improved and as variation in the process is reduced. Productivity improves as you reduce the time spent on rework and working on the wrong things—provided you measure and capture the gains.

We define waste as the difference between the way things are now and the way they could or should be if everything were perfect.

Waste shows itself in four forms—waste of materials, waste of capital, waste of time, and waste from lost sales or other opportunities. All four forms derive from the ineffective use of human talent.

Besides getting the job done, attacking the waste is a great rallying point for the continuous improvement effort. Waste is everywhere—in all areas and all activities. People can understand the need to eliminate waste to be competitive and move towards "world class". When you attack the waste, you are not attacking individuals, but the system that allows the waste to be generated.

When management takes responsibility for the system, it takes responsibility for the waste. Waste is caused by what we work on and how we work. Often more than half the waste results from working on the wrong things—wrong products, wrong markets, wrong technology, etc. And the people responsible for determining the basic mission of the organization and what activities will accomplish that mission and vision are also responsible for most of the waste that results from working on the wrong things. These responsible people should continually examine the focus of the organization's efforts. By doing this early on, they can avoid the huge restructuring efforts or "reengineering" many organizations have recently undergone to change the focus of what to work on. Management takes the lead in finding the really big sources of waste, such as working on the wrong products or investing in the wrong technology. But since managers do not see all the waste, they need the help of all the people working in the system to find the waste, quantify it and eliminate it.

Most people have no idea of the amount of waste in their organizations. This is particularly true of managers and executives, because they are not close to the work processes where the waste is generated, and they are blind to the waste in their own work as they cause waste in the rest of the organization. We see this every week in our seminars and workshops. Historically people have searched for waste primarily in manufacturing, where it is relatively easy to see and measure in the form of scrap or poor productivity. The greatest waste today in most organizations does not originate in manufacturing, yet manufacturing waste is still a huge problem, even though management has focused on it for many years. The biggest wastes are at the interfaces between people and organizations and the interstices between products, technologies, etc. Much waste has not been uncovered because managers have not asked and listened to the people doing the work. They have not asked the right questions. They have not released the power of all the people through imagineering, creativity and innovation.

There is even more waste in the non-manufacturing areas, the so-called white collar areas which now represent nearly three-fourths of all work. Since a great deal of effort is usually expended in reducing scrap and increasing manufacturing productivity, managers and executives tend to feel they are doing all they should to eliminate waste. When a large group of chief executives of large companies was surveyed as to the waste in their companies, they estimated that it averaged about 5% of sales. How differently they might act if they realized it was consuming 20-50% of sales!

Waste is present in all work processes. It occurs in all kinds of organizations and at all levels. It results from the work of directors, executives, managers, front-line employees, government, suppliers and customers. The problems and wasteful activities are part of the system that has grown over the years. They have become a way of doing business. People have been walking by the waste without seeing it every day in the boardrooms, the field sales offices, the laboratories, the plants, the warehouses, everywhere. People must learn to look at waste differently to "see" it. The biggest waste is almost always from the key processes controlled by the top and senior management. That is why the leaders should always be looking for the major management directed programs, the reengineering to change key business processes.

Once you begin to discover how much waste there is, you will develop a new way of thinking, a new consciousness of waste in all its forms, everywhere. When you see how pervasive it is, it becomes obvious that it doesn't need to be there. It's **intolerable**! It's keeping you and your organization from achieving the success you're capable of achieving. To improve continuously, continuously search for and eliminate waste. Study an area, study yourself, and what you discover will start you toward an intolerance for waste. Waste is robbing your organization. You are a P. O. W. (Prisoner of Waste). Since other organizations may be ahead of you in rooting out waste, you have to develop quickly the attitude of waste as the enemy, the opposing team, the obstacle between you and your goals. The search for waste becomes a part of your thinking every day and every hour. Knowing what the waste is energizes the organization and tells you what to work on.

Leaders should be the first to change their behavior, basing their thought, work, talk and actions on continuous improvement through attacking the waste. Take every opportunity to spread this thinking throughout the organization. This is the real culture change!

Change in culture does not come easily, but once a critical mass of people begins to think and act this way, the focus on waste spreads rapidly. People who see what it can do become enthusiastic, and that enthusiasm is contagious. The real desired culture is—everyone works towards common goals to identify, quantify, and eliminate the waste through continuous process improvement—forever!

Waste in all its forms is much more prevalent than people

realize. We estimate that it <u>runs between 20-50% of sales revenue</u> in Western companies. It is usually less in a distribution organization. Practically all organizations have big waste due to the lack of real supplier and customer relationships and partnerships when appropriate. Waste drains so many resources because people cannot or do not recognize most of the waste. Identifying the waste is not easy, but it is critical to the whole process of continuous improvement.

FINDING THE WASTE

First look at the waste in the organization as a whole—from a macro level. This step helps to convince people, including senior management, that the effort is worthwhile.

Typically management establishes an entity, sometimes called a steering committee or quality council, to guide the whole process of adopting the new management model. The makeup of the entity sends a strong message to the organization as to the importance of the process of change and management's commitment to it. This team should include the top leaders, the senior management team, of the company—or its division, department, or other business unit. The senior quality person should also be included as well as a representative from human resources. If there is a union willing to work together with management, give strong consideration to having a union representative on the team. If all major constituencies are represented, people are more likely to accept the need for change. The most effective committee size is five to ten people, depending upon the size of the organization.

Waste at the Interfaces and Interstices

The biggest wastes or opportunities usually occur at the hand over points or interfaces between people, groups, departments, business units, organizations. These big wastes also occur at the interstices–the chinks or gaps between products, ideas, processes, technologies or services. Both of these areas represent enormous opportunities for improvement and these are the places where we should constantly search for the big gains or "ELEPHANTS". We borrow the term "ELEPHANTS" from the oil industry in which they call the giant oil fields, the areas of huge opportunity, the "ELEPHANTS".

Many of us have been using the customer/supplier relationship to search for waste at some of the interfaces. The use of the customer/supplier concept and associated tools have led us to the major wastes that occur when customers and suppliers, internal and external, do not regularly communicate their needs, wants, problems, errors, complexities, or ideas. Examples include the following:

1. Supervisors/Managers and direct reports.
2. Senior management and operating groups.
3. External customers/consumers to the stockholders, Boards of Directors, CEOs, senior management teams, etc.
4. Individuals or groups doing work for the next individual or group in the office, plant, lab, etc.
5. Sales departments to marketing, planning, manufacturing, purchasing, and other groups to where they have important input.

Think of the enormous waste that occurs in many organizations due to the five examples listed above. The following provides more information on each of the above examples.

1. The people doing the work know the real problems and frequently the causes of the problems but they do not tell the management. Some reasons might be the lack of amnesty, lack of past management interest, poor employee relations, or historic "us vs. them" attitudes.

2. The senior management of the organization and operating groups know that major process and work changes are

needed to achieve competitive or world class costs. However, operating groups have learned that it is high risk for them to take the initiative for a major technology change, or a large reduction in the work force through restructuring or reengineering. Another major risk area might be to eliminate major annual or bi-annual, repairs/ rebuilds through improved work practices or equipment changes. (If the operating group initiates the changes, they take the risks, if things don't work out as planned.) And let's face it, the risk may not be minimal. If they wait for the senior management to order changes, then senior management takes the risks.   How many delays for necessary changes do you think are caused by this men- tality? Think of the giant wastes in this area for some major old line industries!

3. Remember the waste of time between the US automobile customers/consumers demanding small cars and the reac- tions of the Board of Directors, CEOs, and operating managers of General Motors, Ford and Chrysler. Many people in those jobs knew that rapid, urgent changes were needed. Yet, there was a delay of 5-10 years before urgent, broad-based work even started! The inability or unwillingness to listen to others, or to admit to others that serious errors in judgment occurred or to take risks—and the general lack of "truth telling" as well as other factors prevented the urgently needed decisions and actions.

4. How often do we see the lack of cooperation hurt an organization? People work in their own silo or stovepipe. They work hard but they do not communicate and work effectively with others towards common goals. They sub- optimize.   They sometimes do not use the customer/ supplier relationship even though they have been educated and trained to do so. Frequently, the reason is the historic

working relationship or lack of it between the groups or people.

5. We see communication problems regularly. The history of "doing your own thing." The Management by Objective System - "I have my objective—I met mine; good luck to you" syndrome. Such systems as practiced in many organizations tend to keep people in their own "stove-pipes" and "silos." The reason is not bad people. It is ineffective management systems, processes, practices that prevent these people from working together.

We see these same problems in government. The lack of proper customer/supplier relationships and the lack of work at the interface, prevent progress. Politics add serious problems to getting things done. Alignment/Common goals can make a big difference in eliminating or reducing these silo mentalities.

In a similar way that the interfaces cause major troubles in most organizations, we see problems at the interstices - the gaps. This was brought to my attention by an aunt of my daughter-in-law, Ann. In 1976, I had helped my son Jim in his decision to become an entrepreneur as an office copy dealer. Several years later, the business was off to a successful start. At a family wedding, the aunt thanked me for providing that help. I quickly gave the credit to my son. The aunt, however, reminded me with the words, "Bill, you were a main part of identifying the opportunity at the interstices in the market. You saw the gap at the meeting point of the Xerox machines and other technologies." I never forgot her lesson. She saw and understood the importance of where to look for the big opportunities.

In newspapers and magazines and on television, we read about the telecommunications business and the information high-way. We are seeing the opportunity at the interstices of the technologies and markets of the computer, telephone, television and other allied businesses. The opportunities are rampant.

Similar opportunities also exist in education, law, health care, biotechnology and other areas for the same reason. There are many major gaps and the gaps represent areas of huge opportunities and potential difficulties.

Think of the tectonic plates by which we ride on the surface of the earth. When the tectonic plates meet, the result is earthquakes, the rising mountain ranges, the volcanic mountains blowing their top. We see what can happen at the interstices. Look at the damage that hurricanes, cyclones, tsunamis, and northeasters do along the shorelines—the meeting place of the land and the oceans.

What do we do about the interstices in our organizations?

Unfortunately many of us see the hurricanes or tsunamis on a regular basis! But it is at these gaps that the huge opportunities lie.

By acknowledging and understanding these factors, we can greatly expand the opportunities that we find and quantify—over and above that we now find from conventional searches for waste. Remember practically all improvement comes from organizations and people trying to close the gaps between current reality and the way things can be.

Boundaries

Boundaries, which are an essential element of the search for waste, can be a double-edged sword. Boundaries are, by definition, limits. When we search for waste, we typically establish boundaries in order to define the area in which to search.

The boundaries we set tell people where to focus their attention, which in turn gets them started more quickly. Boundaries can also help ensure that searches don't deteriorate into "squawk sessions" where everyone points to someone else or to influences outside their control.

Unfortunately, boundaries can also effectively limit the waste that is found - by limiting the processes and systems that are looked at.

To see what I mean, consider the boundaries that might be set for a research laboratory.

1) The search will be for waste which the laboratory manager and people can identify, quantify, and eliminate or reduce. In other words, only waste that is under the control of individuals in the lab. Evidence of such waste includes:

   - products that are too costly for the market due to laboratory specifications for materials, equipment, processes, and/or products
   - products requiring capital investment in lab equipment exceeding $250,000; or requiring two years to develop; or requiring in excess of $1 million in capital equipment, including test equipment for manufacturing
   - work on the wrong things within an assigned project - for example, making minor improvements in products when drastic technological change that yields lower cost and improved customer benefits is required
   - waste in the laboratory that results from lack of communication with suppliers, or that occurs because suppliers are not meeting specifications for materials, equipment, or technical work

2) The search will focus on waste of time and waste of material in the laboratory. On the surface, it would appear that narrowly defining the boundaries gives the laboratory employees clear direction for getting started.

However, setting these boundaries also means that sources of huge waste can go unnoticed or that tremendous opportunities are missed. That is because boundaries often fail to take into account interfaces with other groups and how "dropped balls" or communication breakdowns create waste. Boundaries may also fail to consider the waste that results from an organization's failure to seize opportunities, to identify and close the gaps or interstices in a market.

So, while not establishing boundaries will result in lack of direction and hamper progress, setting boundaries that are too narrowly defined will limit the effectiveness of the search.

The issues then are: How do we select boundaries? Who participates in the selection process? And when should boundaries be breached?

The Who

First, involve key people in the area under discussion. That means including individuals from other areas that affect your group's performance. These can be internal or external customers, internal or external suppliers, and representatives from purchasing, information systems, marketing, warehousing, distribution, manufacturing, or advertising.

The actual make-up of the group deciding on boundaries will vary with the area under study. In some cases, there may be no need for individuals outside the area to be involved, while in other cases you may need involvement from several areas.

Selecting Appropriate Boundaries

Once you've decided on the make-up of the group, you can begin determining which boundaries are appropriate. Start by listing the areas in which your group wants to search. Then make a separate list of the areas in which you do not want to search. Now, list the reasons why you do not want to search in those areas. Test those reasons with key people to assess their validity. This exercise helps everyone focus on selecting the right boundaries for the right reasons.

Overriding Boundaries

This may be the most important consideration regarding boundaries. The biggest sources of waste often are found at the interfaces and interstices - and are not addressed because of boundaries that management has selected.

If the principal source of substantial waste is located outside the boundary, it indicates that management needs to reconsider that boundary. Sometimes a boundary is set because of political, social, or business constraints that prevent a group from dealing with others in the organization. These "sacred cows" can stand in the way of real progress. It may be in the best interest of the organization to breach such boundaries. If a legitimate reason exists for what may appear to be an arbitrary boundary, people need to understand what that reason is.

Rethinking Boundaries

Rethinking boundaries can lead to real progress. Following are three situations to illustrate this point.

The first two show how establishing arbitrary boundaries can block the search for waste. The third example shows how looking at boundaries with a critical eye can be the turning point in finding and eliminating waste.

Situation # 1 R&D Unit of Major Corporation: 500-person unit (including more than 100 people with PhD's); total R&D division budget of $80 million (average cost per person of $100,000).

Boundary: look primarily at waste of R&D people's time.

Problem: In reality, the biggest sources of waste were the process of selecting projects to work on, and the process for stopping or re-directing projects. The underlying cause was that people were working on the wrong things. However, because top management's instructions were to look at waste of time in the R&D laboratory, people were afraid to tackle the problem of working on the wrong things.

Situation # 2 Oil refinery: Major oil refining company with associated chemical operations.

Boundary: Division management focuses on its own operations. The chemical business searches for waste in the chemical company and its customers; the refiner searches for waste and opportunities within its own area and its external market through the oil company's marketing division.

Problem: Studies showed that the greatest waste resulted from the failure to work together to ensure that the quality of the refinery's output and its delivery capabilities meet the chemical division's needs. The chemical division consumes 20%-50% of the refinery's production, yet no one was searching for waste at the interface between the two. Turf protection, jealousy, management by objectives, the ranking system, etc., were getting in the way.

Situation #3 Photo-finishing mail order business: Rising postage rates were eating into profitability. A 40% reduction in mail costs was required in order to build growth in the business.

Boundary: The boundary in this case was mental. Everyone felt that efforts to reduce costs were futile: "It's outside of our control. We can't do anything about it."

Solution: The marketing manager broadened the scope of the search to include a full understanding of the inner-workings of the US mail system. By collecting hard facts and data, the team was able to find out how to reduce postage costs by more than 40%.

Working on the Wrong Thing

The largest source of waste is working on the wrong thing. Since senior management determines priorities for work, their review of what things to work on is critical. While it is important for people from all levels to suggest ideas and work on improvement, certain things can only be started and/or supported from the top level.

- Only top and senior management can work on supplier partnerships, which can yield substantial savings and improved product quality.
- Management decides on the rate and location of expan-

sion, and the size and type of plants, warehouses, stores and office buildings.

- Management determines how people are treated and how to make them partners in continuous improvement.
- Although anyone can come up with good ideas for attacking waste, only management can commit the resources— the time, money, and expertise—to undertake many of the larger projects necessary to get rid of waste.
- Management usually makes decisions about technology.
- Corporate management controls pricing, advertising, the services and products provided, etc.

It is management's responsibility to insure the organization is working on the right things—right products, right markets, right technology, etc.

Major Corporate/Business Unit Processes are Usually the Trouble

Major corporate/business unit processes are usually the trouble. We frequently hear clichés when people talk about improvement or quality. Often used statements are: "it's the process"; "it's the system"; "it's the way we do it"; "just fix the process and everything will be all right." The hard fact is that if we want great results and want to keep them, we need to measure both the process (or system) and the results.

When referring to discrete processes/systems at the lower, middle and upper levels of the organization, most people including top/senior managers use the word process or system. They are usually not thinking of the "big" major systems that often control an organization's destiny that are really the way we run the business.

Searching for Waste from Different Perspectives

The quickest way to move top and senior management into action is to have them identify and quantify the waste in their organization as specifically as they can.

Since waste can be looked at from many angles, we use several ways to search for the waste.

We will discuss five approaches for studying what an organization works on, and how it does that work.

The *Follow the Market, Technology, Competition Approach* reviews product lines, markets, technology, how people are treated, how the organization is capitalized—the basic assumptions as to what the organization is designed to do and how it should operate.

The *Follow the Money Approach* searches for and quantifies waste by examining financial and accounting reports. Part of this search may be studying the cost of quality, including quality control costs and failure of control cost, and the huge waste from lost sales and other lost opportunities.

The *Follow the Systems/Processes Approach* searches for waste in the operating systems and processes of the organization.

The *Follow the People Approach* asks people throughout the organization to identify problems and potential improvement, tapping the brain power and experience of everyone in the organization. This approach should also extend to asking customers and suppliers for suggestions.

The *Follow the Time Approach* focuses on searching for the waste of time—time of people, machines, computers, and time-consuming processes such as product development.

All of these approaches provide a new way to search for the waste. Which approach is best to use first varies with the organization, but we have found that the most effective way to move people into action quickly is usually to use the Follow the Money Approach. This is effective because it shows dramatically the large amount of money to be saved and made by eliminating the waste. It provides an incentive to do the difficult work required.

Follow the Market, Technology, Competition

This approach asks one basic question: "Are we working on the right things?" Working on the wrong things causes more than

50% of the waste in most organizations! The macro approach looks at the overall picture—the entire industry, market, product line, technology, competitive environment, etc.

A good way to begin the macro approach is for a steering committee to ask questions such as:

- Are we in the right business?
- Do our products and/or services please customers?
- Are costs and expense structures competitive?
- What is our productivity? What should it be?
- What are our sales per employee? What could they be?
- Are we using the best technologies?

Information from market research and imagineering can also help to uncover major changes to consider.

These major changes, which attack the waste that comes from working on the wrong things, could include the following:

- change the product (design, appeal, function, etc.)
- change the market approach
- change the technology
- change the machines, equipment, computer systems
- combine, move, or eliminate processes, plants, offices, departments
- change the location of some of the work to a different country or state
- change the major methods
- obtain new equipment, new plant, etc.
- do not do some of the work at all—out-source, sell a business
- do some work as a by-product of another process
- change suppliers
- change your supplier's process, equipment, or technology
- add other new approaches to all or part of your business.

What a "macro" change is depends upon the working level. The changes listed above are appropriate for the steering committee. People at all levels should consider macro changes in the way they do their work. What may be a minor change for the steering committee may be a very major change for someone operating a specific process.

Follow the Money

To use this approach, identify and quantify on a macro level the four forms of waste—waste of material, capital, time, and lost sales opportunities. This assessment doesn't have to be thorough, but it needs to be specific enough to convince people that the big waste is really there. When you use this information to select projects and processes for improvement, you will need more complete information. Identifying waste means uncovering an opportunity for improvement. The greater the waste you identify, the greater the opportunity. We believe that this approach is the most effective way to move people into action.

Follow the Systems/Processes

This approach examines the organization's major systems and processes. The systems approach studies various forces and their effect on one another and the results. Study such systems as production control, order entry and billing, inventory, accounts receivable, performance reviews, pay scales, job promotions, the hiring process, shipping, distribution, purchasing, and engineering design. Look for unneeded complexity, duplication of effort, and effectiveness in meeting customers' needs. If you were starting this business from scratch today, how and where would you do the work or would you have others do this work? Determine the objective(s) of each major system. Is there a better, cheaper, or faster way to accomplish that objective? Are all the systems operating with adequate coordination with other systems (including customers' and suppliers') so that all objectives support each other, rather than conflict? Do the systems support or interfere with continuous improvement—both major process and incremental change?

Follow the People

This approach is critical for getting the most from the continuous improvement effort, particularly the incremental improvements. It involves gathering and acting on the ideas of all the people at all levels involved in the work processes, since they know where the waste is located.

Two ingredients are needed—a management commitment to listen to the people who do the work and a system of communication that encourages people to develop and present their ideas about the waste. These ingredients cannot be developed overnight. People will respond when they realize that their ideas are taken seriously and are acted upon. Don't begin a massive campaign to bring in ideas about waste from all areas until you are organized to respond to those ideas. People will soon stop contributing if they find that no one is paying any attention to their ideas and concerns.

Follow the Time

Time is the raw material of work, so studying the time in detail is an important way to find the waste. This approach is so important that Appendix A is devoted to a discussion of how to study the time in detail.

Estimating the Waste of Capital

The waste of capital includes any working assets you have that you would not need if everything ran right: capital used for inventory, accounts receivable, machinery and equipment, plant, space, etc.

Let's take a company with sales of $100,000,000, and total assets of $50,000,000. Simplified financial statements look something like the balance sheet on the next page.

Balance Sheet

Assets

Cash	$ 1,000,000
Accounts receivable	17,000,000
Inventory	16,000,000
Machinery and equipment	12,000,000
Land and Buildings	4,000,000
Total Assets	$ 50,000,000

Liabilities

Accounts Payable	$ 5,000,000
Bank Loan at 8%	10,000,000
Long term debt at 9%	15,000,000
Stockholders' equity	20,000,000
Total liabilities	$ 50,000,000

Income Statement

Sales	$100,000,000
Less Cost of Goods Sold	65,000,000
Gross Margin	35,000,000
Less expenses	30,000,000
Pre-tax profit	$ 5,000,000

What capital do you really need? With sales of $100,000,000, and accounts receivable of $17,000,000, this company takes an average of just over two months to collect its money. [Divide the annual sales by 12 months: 100,000,000÷12 = $8,333,333 if people paid at 30 days. Now divide current receivables by 1 month receivables to figure how long it takes customers to pay. (17,000000 ÷ 8,333,333 = 2.04 months).] Assume its terms are net payment due in 30 days. Just getting everyone to pay within 30 days instead of 2 months would cut the receivables in half and free up $8,500,000 of capital.

This company has inventory sufficient for about 90 days. Every company is different, but what would the inventory be if everything were right? If there were virtually no work-in-process inventory between processing steps? If the material were immediately shipped to customers when completed? I have seen large manufacturing companies with complex processes reduce their inventory to 20 days or less. If we set 20 days as our target (it could be much lower), the waste is $12,400,000 tied up in inventory unnecessarily.

Here's the calculation: Cost of Goods Sold is $65,000,000. Divide $65,000,000 by 360 days. The result is the cost of the goods that we need to have on hand for 1 day of sales, $180,000. If our inventory target is 20 days, then $180,000 X 20 days = $3,600,000 (this is the amount of inventory that we would have for 20 days worth).   The excess inventory is $16,000,000 - $3,600,000 or $12,400,000.

How closely is the machinery and equipment running to theoretical capacity?   A typical company that has plenty of business will often run at about 60% of theoretical capacity, because of bottlenecks, scheduling problems, maintenance problems, etc. Let's pick 95% of theoretical capacity as the ideal for our company. This means our company has 95%-60% = 35% or $4,200,000 of plant and equipment that it doesn't really need.

With less equipment and less inventory, our company probably has 35% - 45% too much space, at a value of $1,600,000. (40% of land and buildings $4,000,000 [from the balance sheet] = $1,600,000.)

Let's add up the waste of capital. (This is money invested in unnecessary things, not a measure of earnings.)

Accounts receivable	$ 8,500,000
Inventory	12,400,000
Machinery and equipment	4,200,000
Land and buildings	1,600,000
Total Waste of capital	$ 26,700,000

Since the total corporate debt is $25,000,000, eliminating 90% of the waste of capital would enable the company to pay off almost all of the bank loan and the long term debt. If they paid off both the bank loan and the long term debt, they would save interest costs of $2,150,000. (8% of $10,000,000 bank debt = $800,000 plus 9% of $15,000,000 long term debt = $1,350,000 for a total of $2,150,000.) Also, it would save certain inventory carrying costs, such as damage and obsolescence. The company can't get rid of the wasted capital right away, but this estimate shows the opportunities to save capital.

Estimating the Waste of Material

Any material that a company purchases but does not subsequently ship to a customer represents waste (an opportunity for saving). A rough estimate can be made of the physical quantity of raw materials purchased versus the physical quantity of finished goods shipped, adjusted for changes in inventory. This estimate may not be easy to make or accurate in many situations, but it represents a much more inclusive definition of waste than if you just look at material scrapped.

Another source of material waste is lack of partnerships and good communications with suppliers. In a good customer-supplier relationship, both parties work together to provide consistent quality at the lowest cost. They jointly develop specifications which ensure they meet the customer's needs while making optimum use of the supplier's capability. They avoid over- and under-specification.

A typical company may waste as much as 20% of the raw materials it purchases. Assuming raw materials represent 60% of the cost of goods, the waste in our company would be 20% of 60% of $65,000,000, or $7,800,000.

Estimating the Waste of Time

This is difficult to do on a macro basis, because for reasonable accuracy, you need an extended period of work sampling. In a typical organization, people spend their time as shown in the following pie chart.

The Way We Work

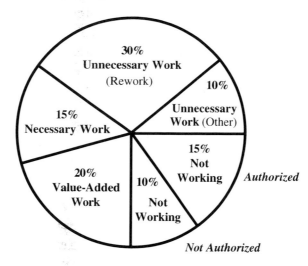

This chart shows that the time spent on unnecessary work (including rework) and unauthorized time not working totals 50%. This does not even include any inefficiencies and ineffectiveness in the value-added and necessary work. Assuming the total payroll cost for this company is $40,000,000, the opportunity for improvement is probably as much as 50% of that or $20,000,000. Once people do work sampling studies on their own work, they begin to believe this.

The cost of wasted time looms even larger when you consider that it is not only people's time that is wasted. Other costly wasted time includes the hours when machines, computers, plants or buildings are idle and the time that energy is used but not required.

Estimating the Waste from Lost Sales and Other Opportunities

This is the hardest waste to estimate, but usually the biggest waste of all. Remember that it is here that we obtain growth in sales, earning market share and jobs. Imagine how your people feel when they see all the job slashing with little action taken and little investment for job creation. Look at your market share in various areas and/or for various products and services. What could it be? Estimate how your salespeople spend their time. What percent is value-added work? How much more could you sell if new products and services came out on a more timely basis? What would happen to your sales if you had no customer complaints, if the quality were always perfect and if you had no returns or allowances? What if your costs and prices were the lowest in the industry and you had the best possible distribution? What if you developed products and services so that you always had the right product or service at the right time? What could your market share be?

Every company is different, but for our typical company, sales could easily be increased by 20%, or $20,000,000. The added pre-tax profit from these incremental sales would approximate the gross margin of 35% or $7,000,000. (35% of $20,000,000 = $7,000,000)

There are usually lots of other opportunities for profit improvement, which I will discuss later, but at this point they are too difficult to estimate to include in the first macro waste estimate.

Total Opportunity for Increasing Pre-Tax Profit

Add the opportunities for eliminating waste:

Material	$ 7,800,000
Capital	2,150,000
Time of People	20,000,000
Lost Sales	7,000,000
Total Profit/Loss Opportunity	$ 36,950,000

This opportunity to reduce waste totals more than 35% of gross sales of the company! Such savings may seem impossible, but we estimate that the average Western manufacturing company's waste is about 40% of gross sales and many of the country's leading business executives now agree.

When making the macro waste study, 100% accuracy is not important. What is important is to gain a consensus that there is a large difference between the way the organization is operating and the way it would operate if everything were perfect. This difference means that there is a large opportunity, worth a massive effort. Also, if people believe the approximate figures, they can see where the largest waste areas are. Combine those estimates with a judgment as to how difficult the improvements will be in each area, and you have a guide to set your priorities.

MOVE INTO ACTION AND DEVELOP A PLAN

The next phase consists of two parallel activities—planning and action. Eventually you will need a quality plan, including a vision and mission for the organization. Below is Conway Quality's Quality Planning Process.

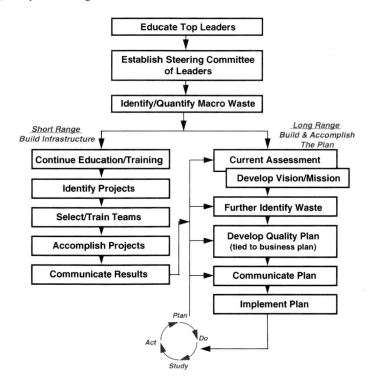

In my experience, doing all of the planning first is not effective. You will make more mistakes, and those mistakes will be widespread. You will waste time getting started. The change in behavior is the most important goal, and just publicizing a plan does not alter behavior or change the organization's culture. Before completing a continuous improvement plan, a considerable amount of "doing" is required as a part of management's education and training. Follow the Shewhart cycle of "Plan, Do, Study, Act." Start out by developing a short term—six months to a year—plan to get going. During that period develop a more complete, longer-term quality plan.

Initial Projects

Do things on a small then a medium sized scale before making a grand plan. The system of continuous improvement is so different and so powerful, that merely reading and talking about it does not suffice. Immediately following their education and training, people need to start off with small but meaningful projects. Small projects will give them a chance to make mistakes as they learn without having highly visible failures. They will probably have to involve others in their project(s), but if everyone understands that it is a trial project, and a learning experience, mistakes will do no lasting harm. Success convinces people of the power of the system, and they can then provide leadership to others with more credibility and enthusiasm. Then they can move people into action and help them be successful in attacking the waste. That success leads to changed behavior. Selecting good initial projects and implementing them well are critical to move the process in the right direction. Undertake a limited number to insure that sufficient resources can be available to execute those few projects aggressively. These initial projects should be:

- Small, but meaningful
- Short-term (one to three months)
- Likely to succeed.

Once people are educated in the continuous improvement process, they will have a high degree of interest in the first projects. They will want to see if the system really works. The reasonable success of most of these early projects is critical to gain momentum for the process. The projects should begin to show some results in a relatively short period—not longer than three months. The results should be measurable against an objective standard.

Some initial projects I have seen work successfully are:

- Reduce material waste and/or rework in a particular process
- Identify reasons for back orders and begin to eliminate them
- Reduce average waiting time
  - at checkout counters
  - in teller lines
  - in drive-through lanes at a restaurant
  - at copy machines
  - for response to service requests
  - in an emergency room
  - for telephone to be answered
- Reduce make-ready time for a critical process
- Reduce invoice pricing errors
- Reduce time between product shipment and mailing of invoice
- Reduce time between customer payment and application of cash
- Identify reasons for late delivery and begin to eliminate them
- Evaluate and reduce need for courier services to deliver paperwork or product
- Increase percentage of steam condensate returned to boiler
- Reduce volume of hazardous waste

- Reduce travel time for salespeople and increase number of calls per day
- Reduce the number of reports and reduce the number of people receiving the remaining ones
- Reduce the number of meetings and the time spent in each
- Devise ways to get more business from existing customers
- Streamline sales reporting requirements
- Review the process for developing qualified sales leads
- Improve utilization of hospital operating room and X-ray equipment
- Reduce patient waiting time in emergency room, in lab, for X-rays
- Reduce response time for maintenance workers to arrive at machine
- Insure maintenance workers arrive at machines with needed tools
- Reduce errors in entering orders

Most of these projects involve eliminating waste of time or material. These types of projects are usually less complex than eliminating waste of capital and discovering lost opportunities. You can select projects that have easily measurable results and that help people learn to use the tools of continuous improvement. Most of these projects are local. They are done where the manager has control of the key processes. As the organization has success, gradually work starts on the cross department projects.

Project Teams

Project teams need clear project objectives; teams need an effective leader—one who has a participatory style and is comfortable operating as a player/coach. The leader should be respected by other members of the team and be enthusiastic about continuous improvement. Team members should be people working in, or with experience in, the area being studied, or customers or suppliers of the process.

Facilitators

Assign a facilitator/trainer to each team if necessary. Identify training needs for the particular project and provide training to the team just prior to the start of the project and when additional training needs become apparent. The project should have a sponsor with sufficient authority to provide the resources needed and to ratify any decisions made. The sponsor may not be an actual member of the team, but he/she should follow the project closely, show a high degree of interest, and be prepared to clear any roadblocks.

Give any significant success immediate publicity throughout the organization. The best way to build support for the system is for people to see what it can achieve. Achievement brings the motivation to do more.

The cycle—move into action, develop joy in achievement, develop motivation to do more, move further into action—is underway.

In addition to being sponsors for teams, several, if not all, of the people on the steering committee should be involved in projects, either as team members, as leaders, or on their own. This kind of involvement does two things: 1) it gives leaders experience with the tools and processes of the system and 2) it sends a message that this is a system that everyone will be using.

After the initial or pilot projects begin to show some success, gradually expand training and project work at a rate that is sustainable with the resources available. As teams become more experienced, they can take on new projects with less support. The eventual goal is to have all people sufficiently trained and experienced to participate in project work with less staff support. As people gain confidence and experience, the projects gradually expand into those of greater difficulty and size, including cross-department projects and eventually major management innovation or reengineering.

Any organization that begins and sustains continuous improvement needs to strive to be a Learning Organization. Part of that learning includes these few items for ongoing education and training:

Education
- Review of the four forms of waste and the five ways to search for waste, including the questions to ask. For instance, the opportunities in supplier partnerships are now much greater than most people believed even two to three years ago.
- Proper balance between internal and external customers...the external customer must come first
- How to use the Value Added Work concept to improve any kind of work

Training
- Training and education for all new employees
- "Just in time" refresher training for project teams on statistical tools, collecting and analyzing data, and working in teams
- Refresher training for senior managers on key items each year

CHAPTER 3
PLAN, PROMOTE, ASSESS

THE QUALITY PLAN (or THE MANAGEMENT PLAN FOR IMPROVEMENT)

The quality plan is really the management's plan to improve continuously. After the initial project work begins, the steering committee starts to develop this management plan. Although some of the work may be delegated to sub-committees or others, the steering committee itself will usually undertake the initial planning responsibilities.

1) Establish awareness, education and training programs
2) Provide facilitators where needed
3) Provide other resources needed
4) Develop communications and publicity programs (provide for a reporting system)
5) Assess the organization's current position
6) Develop, define and share the organization's mission, vision, values and beliefs. (See Chapter 4.) Get suggestions from all areas of the organization
7) Set objectives—the vital few
8) Further identify waste
9) Identify key programs to be directed by management
10) Review the human relations practices, procedures and culture of the organization as they relate to the continuous improvement system and start taking action
11) Review the system of relationships with customers and suppliers

As the quality management plan for Continuous Improvement develops, it will become part of the overall Strategic Plan of the business and also part of the Business Plan. Gradually the three will become one—a plan for a way to run the business now and in the future.

We can see that without integration of these plans we will have conflict with what we work on. How can we have real alignment and common purpose without it? We cannot. Think of it this way—waste varies in organizations from 20-50% of revenue averaging 30-40%. It is clear then that eliminating this waste has to be part of all these plans. We can use it to bring the plans together.

A major client company, The Ready Bake Division of Weston Foods, is currently in the process of moving to that goal. Note that the waste is the element that pulls them together.

Each department head brings together representatives from department teams who estimate the waste they currently face. The sources of the waste are quantified and displayed on a Pareto chart. The group votes on what they want to set as their waste elimination target for the upcoming year, and establishes a tentative priority list of what they are going to work on. Finally, they consider what specific training needs exist.

Next, the department heads meet together with the General Manager (who serves as a facilitator). All of the waste, all of the waste targets, all of the priority action plans, and all of the training needs, are literally added together and re-voted on. As a result, everyone has an idea how they contribute to the overall improvement in the division, and how their respective action plans might help or hinder the achievement of improvement in other departments.

Appendix C, "Education and Training for the Revolution," provides suggestions for the kind of detailed plan and schedule a steering committee will typically develop to provide the appropriate education and training programs. Then it can delegate to one person the job of implementing and maintaining the programs and developing trainers and facilitators.

Because of their importance, entire chapters are devoted to items 7 through 11 on the committee's agenda. The rest of this chapter will focus on responsibilities 4, 5, and 6 in the list above.

DEVELOP COMMUNICATION AND
PUBLICITY PROGRAMS

The communication plan should include ways to convince everyone that the organization and its management are serious about changing the culture of the organization. The plan should include not just discussions and other publicity, but also actions by managers that show they are personally committed to make the necessary changes.

Newsletters, group meetings, memos, etc. can help to keep everyone informed of progress. It is especially important that project teams receive recognition as they make significant progress. This is one of the best ways to let people know their active participation is appreciated. Some other ways are:

- Say thank you
- Write a thank you note
- Arrange for a presentation to senior management
- Arrange for stories and updates in the company newsletter
- Include success stories in the annual report
- Distribute case studies on successful projects throughout the organization
- Use success stories in company advertising
- Send out news releases on successes

The steering committee also needs to receive communications from the project teams and others. To maintain spontaneity and avoid having their enthusiasm dampened by bureaucratic restraints, the teams should not be burdened with extensive formalized procedures and reporting, particularly at first. But to avoid wasted motion and duplication, team leaders or their sponsors need to inform the steering committee of their progress, their successes and their failures. Everyone is in a learning stage, and the lessons learned by one team should be communicated to the others.

ASSESS THE ORGANIZATION'S CURRENT POSITION

The steering committee should provide a baseline from which to develop a vision and mission and to measure progress. This will include:

- Amount of waste
- Level of quality
- Competitive position
- Customer satisfaction
- Productivity
- Employee attitudes
- Strengths
- Weaknesses
- Opportunities
- Threats

Many organizations already have a mission and/or vision statement. They have had a two or three day management meeting and have published their mission/vision statement throughout the company. The problem is that the great majority of people read the statement but don't understand how it affects them and their work. They don't feel a "part" of it and are not committed to it. The statement does not achieve its goal of alignment behind a common purpose.

Management should revisit their mission/vision statement with the understanding that it needs to help them eliminate the waste in their organization and serve their customers. Then they need to follow the statement themselves, educate other people to see how it affects them and continually push it until it becomes a way of life for everyone.

Case: Assessment of a Photo Finishing Company

As an example let's study what a steering committee for a

large mail order photo finishing company found during its initial assessment.

Waste of Materials

A project team compared actual use of chemicals, photographic paper and packaging materials with theoretical perfection and found that the company was wasting 13% of the paper, 18% of the chemicals, and 12% of the packaging materials. Further, the team found that the company recovered only 58% of the silver it could have recovered from the used chemical solutions. A study showed that postage costs, for various reasons, exceeded the theoretical cost by 9%.

Waste of Time

Team members examine the theoretical time for processing an order against the actual payroll hours, and discovered that productivity was 70% of what they thought was possible. They also found that a large part of the shortfall was due to difficulty in scheduling staff to match a varying work load.

Waste of Capital

The company had 45 days worth of inventory, although a study showed that 15 days should be sufficient with proper planning and inventory coordination. Capacity studies showed that the company could theoretically process 50% more orders with the present space and equipment.

Lost Opportunities

A study revealed that the company's market share by region varied from 3% to 17%. Also, sales of its own private label film amounted to only 9% of the film received for processing. Finally, its ratio of reprint and enlargement business to film processing was only 63% of the industry average.

Level of Quality of Product and Service
The organization conducted a continuing survey comparing various quality factors with the competition's. Factors surveyed included brightness, density, color balance, neatness of packaging, and turnaround time.

Competitive Position
They evaluated their overall quality, pricing, cost structure, customer service, and market share as compared to the competition's.

Customer Satisfaction
They surveyed their customers to gauge their perception of quality and service. They set up a rating system comparing themselves to their competitors and against theoretical perfection. They asked customers for suggestions about improving service.

Productivity
Starting with the estimate that productivity was 30% lower than what was theoretically possible, they detailed the areas of shortfall and identified the reasons for the shortfall. Some of these reasons were scheduling, inadequate training, equipment problems and erratic mail delivery. They quantified the waste of time in each area.

Employee Attitudes
Through interviews and a written survey, they established a benchmark of employees' attitudes about
- the company
- their job
- working conditions
- management and its willingness to listen
- teamwork
- the importance of satisfying customers

They also asked people what they thought were the major problems and opportunities for the company.

Strengths, Weaknesses, Opportunities and Threats

The management evaluated all of this information, and discussed what they had learned thus far, and evaluated the company's strengths, weaknesses, opportunities and threats. During two days away from the office, an independent facilitator helped them complete their evaluation and develop a statement of why they were in business (their mission) and what they wanted to attain over the next five to seven years (their vision).

A list of their conclusions follows.

Strengths:
- One of the lowest costs in the industry
- Good name recognition among mail order customers
- Strong operations in three countries
- Good series of contracts for distribution of promotional envelopes
- Skilled and flexible work force

Weaknesses:
- Inconsistent quality
- Long delivery times to customers west of the Mississippi
- Weak position selling through dealers
- Poor market share of reprint and enlargement business
- Poor market share of one-time-use camera business

Opportunities:
- Increase market share in weak areas, both product and geographical areas
- Expand to additional countries
- Become lowest cost producer in industry
- Sell additional products to present customers

Threats:
- Filmless digital picture taking with compact disc storage and display
- Less costly video cameras affecting growth of "snap-shots"
- One hour photo shops
- Price reduction by major competitor

In the back of their minds, the steering committee members knew most of these factors. Focusing on the strengths, weaknesses, opportunities and threats (S.W.O.T.) helped them agree on priorities and what needed to be done.

CHAPTER 4
CHOOSE THE VITAL FEW

Once the management team has assessed in detail the organization's current position and begun to develop its improvement through quality plan, they might be tempted to start people working on all the little sources of waste they uncovered, feeling that they had set the continuous improvement process in motion. Many organizations have made this mistake. To a real leader in improvement, every new piece of information, every new plan-in-progress, provides an opportunity to look at the really big questions and lead the really big changes.

WHAT SHOULD WE WORK ON?

The most crucial decision most organizations face is, What should we work on? Companies that have experimented unsuccessfully with quality programs often act as though changes can be made only on the micro level, as though factory-floor quality circles could make all the changes necessary, if only they would work hard enough. I certainly don't underestimate the importance of micro changes, of every person examining and improving his or her own work processes, and much of the rest of this book focuses on changes at a departmental level.

But that should not cloud the fact that the big leaps in quality, growth, effectiveness, efficiency, and profitability most often result from decisions that only top managers can make. In my recent work with a billion-dollar giant retailer, I pointed out that even though the company has thousands of people working at retail locations, top managers can probably eliminate several times as much waste as can store employees. Only top managers can make the decisions that attack major sources of waste.

Only they can:

- Form partnerships with suppliers, arrangements that may reduce costs 5% or more
- Decide on the location of stores and rate of expansion
- Set up systems covering how people are treated, systems which determine whether people choose to apply their skills and expertise to continuous improvement or just get by; these include pay, promotions, and performance reviews
- Make company-wide decisions about pricing, products, services, merchandising, etc.
- Supply people with the resources they need. For example, people working at the checkout counters of a supermarket may know best how to improve their work, but without top management's willingness to do work studies, provide technology, invest capital, and treat the people as experts, people working at the retail level can make only minor improvements.

Overall, I believe that choosing the right things to work on opens up at least half of the improvements that are possible in the continuous improvement system. Many major management directed programs, major process changes, and reengineering projects involve substantial changes in an organization's answer to the question, What should we work on? Therefore, organizations devoted to continuous improvement apply the kind of disciplined examination advocated in this book to:

- Define their vision and mission
- Translate their vision and mission into the Vital Few
- Choose projects on which to focus time and resources
- Plan at all levels, including capital investment and technology changes

DEVELOP AND DEFINE THE ORGANIZATION'S VISION AND MISSION

The purpose of a Vision and Mission is to:

- Help develop a consensus about the organization's reason for being, its goals and objectives. In order to make progress toward a common purpose, people need to be aligned. They all need to be working toward the same goal. I use the shorthand "Hong Kong" to describe a common goal, since I always wanted to go there as a child. If some people want to go to Hong Kong, and some to Paris or Rio de Janeiro, the organization will never get to any of the destinations. Without alignment, progress is severely restricted
- Communicate those aims to everyone in the organization, and to suppliers and customers as appropriate
- Identify and help to focus everyone's efforts toward the "vital few" objectives
- Serve as a basis for a plan of action.

Completing the current assessment outlined in the previous chapter gives a good background for establishing the vision and mission. Discuss the vision and mission immediately after the current assessment to help the management team members focus on the really big issues and connect the question "What should we work on?" to the smaller problems and sources of waste that the assessment identified. Chasing the waste in an organization requires close examination of the smallest elements of work, as we will see in Chapter 7, but everyone, especially top managers, needs to keep one eye on the big issues, the mission and vision, the major waste, the major process to change and improve. What are we trying to do? Where are we going? The Vital Few!

The following diagram shows the process to develop the Vision and Mission. This process is described more fully on pages 182-188 of *The Quality Secret.*

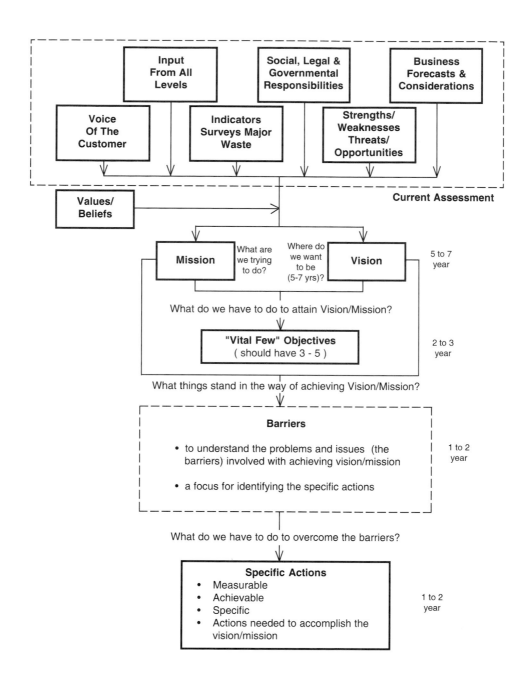

The purpose of this process is to help in developing alignment and common purpose for the entire organization. The process helps us to work on the Vital Few and the projects to carry out the Vision, Mission and Vital Few.

Let us look at a brief description of vision and mission and look at a diagram of the product of our work.

> **Vision**—*a mental image of a desirable, achievable future state. The image is arrived at through imagineering.*

> **Mission**—*a statement of specific activities and projects that people or teams are charged with performing which have a well defined role in achieving the vision and the Vital Few.*

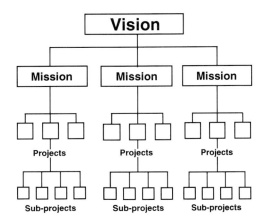

The photo finishing company discussed in Chapter 1 agreed on the vision. It states where they are trying to go.

> *Within six years we will become the world's largest and most profitable, people-oriented mail order photo finishing company with the lowest cost structure and excellent quality and service to please our external customers.*

Notice a key item in their vision is growth, and growth leads to job creation. Continuous process improvement (both major and incremental processes) works much better in a growing organization. The reason is obvious to all—employment security.

The mission then became the following:

Our mission is to provide the best value to the photo finishing customer in terms of low cost and high quality. We will do this by mail order marketing directly to the customer. We will drive down costs by changing and improving the work to eliminate the waste.

This is a seemingly simple statement, but it defines what we will do to work towards the vision. The company's goals are quite measurable. The areas of quality and service require new measuring systems through periodic studies and surveys to see how well it was moving toward these goals. The organization is on its way to Hong Kong.

DEFINE OBJECTIVES

Once the steering committee of the photo finishing company established its vision and mission they needed to decide how to go about reaching these goals. They needed to set a few (three to five) critical objectives and identify any barriers to achieving those objectives.

The photo company established its "vital few" as:

- Find new cost-effective methods of promotion to reach additional segments of the picture-taking population.
- Develop continuous improvement projects that will improve productivity by at least 12% a year for three years.
- Find a way to match more closely the work force with a

widely fluctuating work load caused by variations in picture-taking occasions.

- Refine and eliminate waste in the processes to achieve, and be recognized for, high consistent quality.

Next, the steering committee identified barriers to achieving those objectives. As an example, a barrier to matching the work force to a fluctuating work load was that many current employees wanted full-time work but did not want to work much overtime because of family commitments. The committee then identified two strategic actions to overcome that barrier: it would search for outside work, such as data entry or filling orders for a catalog company, that workers could do in off-peak periods; also, over time, it would find people who wanted to work flexible hours.

FURTHER IDENTIFY WASTE

One more step is needed to identify and set priorities for which areas to work on first: examine the waste in more detail. Studying waste from a macro view gives some initial ideas. Now the waste needs to be broken down into small enough pieces to be attacked with individual projects. After the current assessment, the steering committee will find it easier to think of areas of waste caused by lost opportunities. The next two chapters focus on this step.

IDENTIFY KEY PROGRAMS TO BE DIRECTED BY MANAGEMENT—MAJOR MANAGEMENT IN-NOVATIONS

An important step towards getting the maximum benefits from the continuous improvement process is to identify those projects which:

- are doable
- have the most improvement possibilities

- can be accomplished with the resources available
- are part of the Vital Few

You do not start on these major management directed projects until you have built an infrastructure for working effectively in the new way on small and medium-sized projects. That usually takes 1 to 2 years.

The Continuous Improvement Timeline

The chart below illustrates the continuous improvement timeline and shows the primary Conway Quality products and services that are available to help you at each step of the way.

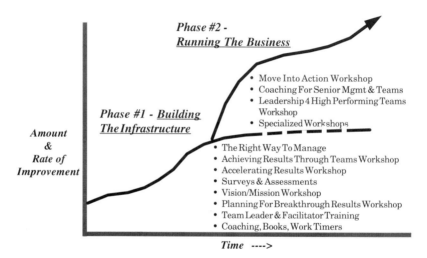

The actual time required to build an infrastructure that will enable you to make major process changes varies with each organization. It depends on your organization's size and complexity, its initial status (i.e., how much improvement is necessary), and top management's commitment to leading change.

Successful work on the infrastructure and progression into Phase 2 enable you to run your business in a vastly improved way. You'll experience quantum gains in customer satisfaction, greater growth, and lower costs. You'll be able to enhance your products' and services' quality and reliability. The results will be evident on your bottom line. You'll find that more opportunities open up for employees. And your organization will be a better place to work.

No organization can do everything at once. Deciding what to work on is critical. Management sets priorities based on the current assessment, the detailed study of waste, and the resources available. The number of projects should be small enough to be manageable and to insure that each project gets the resources required for success. Five to eight projects is a reasonable number to start, for most organizations. If the major management directed programs are very large and substantially all encompassing, then the organization should try to handle only a few at a time. Each project should be assigned a member of management as a sponsor whose responsibility includes:

- Helping to pick a team that will do the job
- Assisting team members in defining the project
- Insuring the team has the necessary training
- Making sure everyone understands the objective(s) of the project and that the objective(s) is measurable
- Providing the resources needed
- Eliminating roadblocks when required
- Generally following the progress to see that the effort stays focused and maintains a reasonable schedule

As the team makes progress, the sponsor should arrange to publicize the successes and provide other recognition for the team.

Other Projects
Eventually each of the original management-directed projects will be completed or become institutionalized so that it is part of the day-to-day responsibilities of the people in charge of the processes involved. Most major projects require sub-projects and sub-sub-projects. Focusing on one major problem or oppor-

tunity soon leads to the development of 10, 50, or 100 problems or opportunities. As a particular management-directed project starts to require less special attention and fewer resources, the organization can focus its time and resources on such sub-projects or on new management-directed projects.

As training and experience become more widespread, spontaneous project teams spring up to attack problems people discover in their areas of work. These are often incremental improvements in contrast to the major process changes that come from the major management directed programs. Such spontaneity should be encouraged, because it is a key part of the cultural change that you want. Eventually, everyone should be working this way every day, not only on projects but also in their regular work. But some control is necessary, so that people do not get ahead of the training or the resources. People forming teams to undertake projects on their own may waste a lot of time, and they may end up frustrated with lack of progress. They may then perceive that the fault is with the continuous improvement system, when it is actually with a lack of training. This often happens when companies form numerous "quality circles" all at once throughout the company. While anyone and everyone can work in continuous improvement, people are not likely to be successful until they understand what continuous improvement is and are trained in the use of the necessary tools.

CHAPTER 5
ORGANIZE PROJECTS

A successful project requires:

- Choice of an appropriate problem or opportunity and agreement by the team that the project will be worthwhile and trust the team is capable of doing it.
- A well-defined objective
- Team members with background and/or experience in the process being studied
- Training for team members in the appropriate technical tools and team skills
- A committed leader
- Necessary support and resources
- A methodology to solve problems or explore opportunities by improving and changing processes.

DEFINE THE OBJECTIVE

The organization should consider each step—from the development of the mission and vision to the implementation of recommendations—in terms of its objectives. What will the next step accomplish, and how will it fit into the larger scheme? A project objective should be measurable but not a fixed figure, since such a goal may set an artificial cap on performance. Typical objectives for management-directed projects are:

- Reduce the waste in process X to or below a level of 3%
- Identify and eliminate causes for customer complaints
- Reduce the cycle time between order receipt and shipment by at least 75%
- Reduce the days outstanding of accounts receivable to raise at least $30,000,000 cash

- Improve the productivity in Process Y by 5% per month at a minimum
- Substantially reduce the time it takes to develop a new product and bring it to market. Aim for a minimum of 70% reduction

While numerical objectives can be limiting, interim goals may be useful. Or you may have an improvement objective, such as increasing productivity by at least X per cent a month. The keys are:

(1) Avoid caps.
(2) Develop a plan to accomplish the objective.
(3) Base objectives on facts, data.

There may be overlap in the projects. Reducing the waste in process X may also improve the productivity and the delivery time. In this case define your most important objective and let the other goals be sub-projects.

A department may participate in management directed programs and/or develop projects of its own. Typical department projects might be:

- Reduce the error rate in processing orders by 90% in six months
- Increase department productivity by at least 3% per month
- Improve the scheduling of work to even out the work load
- Improve response time to customer requests to eliminate customer complaints
- Reduce machine down time to a maximum of 3%
- Provide cross training to improve flexibility and skill levels for at least one extra job for each employee
- Eliminate a bottleneck operation
- Reduce in-process inventory by at least 90% and production time by at least 50% by using just-in-time concepts.

SELECT A TEAM

Pick project team members who have knowledge of and/or experience with different aspects of the process(es) being studied. You also may want someone with some particular expertise applicable to the project. The people who know most about the problems are those working in the process every day. Periodically you may need to bring someone in for special help.

Most project teams have from three to seven people. If you need more than seven people to cover all aspects of the problem, see if the project should be broken into sub-projects.

Select people who have had exposure to the concepts of continuous improvement. Whenever possible, pick those who feel positive about working this way and who work well in teams. Try to include at least one who is a natural leader in the group—one who is willing to drive the project.

TRAIN TEAM MEMBERS

Train people to use the tools they will need for the project if they have not had the training already. Train them just prior to, or during the project, so they will have a chance to apply the tools before they forget the training.

DESIGNATE A LEADER

The team needs a leader, ordinarily the supervisor or manager of the process being studied. In major management directed programs this is a senior manager with required power who can be a leader of change. If the study crosses organizational lines, the supervisor of the group most involved normally acts as leader. However, other factors such as expertise or experience may dictate a different choice. Depending on the project and the experience of team members, senior managers may designate the leader or the team itself may choose one of its members.

ENSURE RESOURCES

Before beginning a project, the leader should ensure that the necessary resources will be available to carry out the project. The resources needed will vary widely. A simple project may not require any outside resources, but sometimes money and/or the time of outside experts may be needed. Implementing the recommendations of a successful project may require funds for new equipment or other purposes. Before starting a project, the project group should reach an agreement with management that if the recommendations meet certain criteria, management will make funds available. We have all heard of the team that completes a project with seemingly logical recommendations and then finds that nothing happens.

USE A FACILITATOR

Although many projects proceed successfully without a facilitator, the project manager should have a facilitator available to call on when needed. The facilitator needs expertise in using the necessary tools and training in team dynamics and meeting skills. During team meetings, the facilitator acts as a neutral outsider and observer. He or she helps evaluate progress and makes suggestions on the process of the meeting (as opposed to content) to the team, including the team leader. Between meetings, the facilitator can provide coaching to the team leader or other team members. If more training is needed, the facilitator suggests an appropriate course, or undertakes training on the spot. The team leader and facilitator work together closely to ensure the team and project succeed.

START SMALL

Realistically, initial projects will not always go smoothly. For most people, working in teams on continuous improvement is a new experience. Many people may not be comfortable with the changes in attitude and thinking required. The best way to generate a positive attitude is to have a successful project, and one way to insure a successful project is to have a positive attitude. To break this chicken-and-egg paradox, part of the training for a major project should be "practice" with a simpler, but still meaningful, project. This develops confidence in the use of the basic tools for continuous improvement. Success in a small project can breed success in subsequent projects. Start with a small "chicken" and eventually you can work up to a large "goose" that lays golden eggs.

REFINE THE OBJECTIVE

Any project, large or small, needs a clear definition of the objective. If management or a sponsor creates a project and assigns the project team, it will usually define the team's initial objective. But the team needs to review, refine, and commit to it. Even before establishing a team, the leader will discuss the objective with the sponsor and potential team members and refine it using their input. This helps to insure a realistic, practical project. It can also help "pre-sell" the idea for the project and aid the leader in identifying potential team members.

The objectives of the first meeting of the team should be to:

- Identify the opportunity
- Explain the objective for the project
- Agree upon the objective and its wording
- Identify potential resources available and needed
- Decide on what data is needed initially and assign people to obtain the data
- Discuss time constraints and scheduling of meetings
- Establish values and guidelines
- Clarify roles of the team members

Case: Project to Reduce Pricing Problems

A company I worked with was getting numerous complaints from customers about invoice pricing errors.   The company started a project, and one of its leaders described the results to me as follows:

The Controller asked the Billing Supervisor, Mary to initiate a project to eliminate invoice pricing errors. After discussing the problem with the people doing the invoicing work, Mary chose Rosa, Dan and Dean to be members of the project team.

First Meeting

At their first meeting, the team established values and guidelines which clarified the way they were going to treat each other. Then they discussed how they thought the project might work. Mary wrote the project objective on an easel: "Eliminate invoice pricing errors." After some discussion, Dean said, "You know some of the errors customers complain about aren't really our errors. Sometimes the customer has an outdated price list, or sometimes the salesperson makes a special price concession and doesn't tell anyone. Maybe we need a broader objective." After some more discussion, they decided the objective should be, "Eliminate reasons for customer complaints about invoice pricing errors."

They also decided that to meet this objective they would need someone from the sales department on their project team. Mary agreed to talk to the Sales Manager about getting a salesperson to come to at least some of the meetings.

Next they discussed what data would be needed for their study. They agreed that the most important information needed was how many complaints were made and what the causes were. They listed the various causes they could think of such as wrong quantity, wrong product code, outdated price list, etc. They designed a quick form so that billing clerks could enter information whenever they received a complaint.

They discussed when and how often they should meet and

identified an action plan. They agreed they would need about a month's data to have enough information to classify the complaints but that they would get together briefly each week to check on progress and resolve any questions. Mary also volunteered to prepare a rough flow chart of the process before the next formal meeting.

Just as the meeting was breaking up, Dan said, "I just had another thought. There must be some invoice errors that don't result in a customer complaint. I'm sure they don't catch everything, or it may be too small for them to bother about. Or it may be in their favor and they might not tell us. We could be losing a lot of money from that." After discussing this comment they agreed to make one more change in the objective: "Eliminate <u>possible</u> reasons for customer complaints about invoice pricing errors." Dan was assigned the job of trying to figure how they could identify pricing errors other than by customer complaints.

Dan had a good point. A competitive organization needs ways to improve products and services before customers complain. Relationships and communication with customers and suppliers can lead to substantial improvement even to processes that didn't seem to have any problems.

Key activities that take place in most first meetings are:
- Introduce members
- Discuss purpose of group and review mission statement
- If needed provide just-in-time training in
    - variation
    - customer/supplier relationships
    - principles of work
    - human relations
- Clarify team roles: team member, team leader, facilitator, scribe
- Agree on ground rules
- Plan initial activities
- Set future meeting dates
- Process check (how did we do?)

Second Meeting
The agenda for the second meeting was:

- Examine data gathered since the first meeting
- Decide what additional data is needed
- Discuss a rough flow chart of the process
- Identify problem areas
- Assign people to investigate causes for specific problem areas
- Discuss the imagineering process and ask people to think about the perfect process before the next meeting
- Discuss contribution of Sales Department to the project

At the second meeting, Mary introduced Bill, a salesperson assigned to help the project team. Then they examined the data they had gathered since the last meeting. Mary had put the data in the form of a Pareto chart, which is shown below.

Reasons for Customer Pricing Complaints

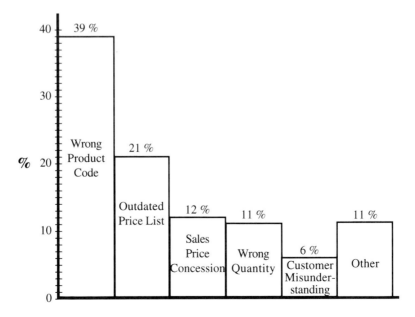

First they discussed the problems that occurred in gathering the data. Rosa pointed out that there were probably some duplication of the complaints. She knew that she and Dan had entered the same complaint in at least four cases, since they had both heard about the cases. They decided that they should continue to gather more data, and the only person to enter the complaint on the form would be the person responsible for answering the complaint. They also agreed to record the invoice number associated with each complaint so they could classify the data further. They decided it might be useful to classify the complaints by size of customer, and by sales territory.

Next, they discussed the two largest causes on the Pareto Chart, "wrong product code," and "outdated price list used." They then divided these two causes into sub-causes. For example, some of the reasons for wrong product codes were customer error, sales correspondent error, and billing clerk error. They further attempted to identify some of the sub-sub-causes of these three types of error.

Mary prepared a rough flow chart of the process. By looking at that chart they could see at what point the problems arose. Some team members commented on errors and omissions in the rough chart, and Mary agreed to revise it before the next meeting.

The team then decided which were the most important problems, and team members volunteered to investigate each of them before the next meeting. Mary said, "We've seen how the process presently works and where some of the problems lie. We're going to do some further investigation of those problems. Before the next meeting I'd like you to think about what the perfect process would look like, one that would be free of all the problems and errors. Then we'll imagineer it together and see where it differs from the present process."

Finally they discussed what was needed from the Sales Department, and the salesperson, Bill, volunteered, "I can see that a lot of these problems come from the sales area. I don't really think I have enough background or authority to resolve all those problems. What I'd like to do is ask the boss if we can start a parallel project in our department. Then I'd be happy to serve as liaison with this team. We might try a broader objective, like 'Eliminate all shipping and invoicing errors caused by the Sales Department.' What do you think?"

Mary replied, "I think that would be great. I've talked to your boss about our project and she's very enthusiastic about it. I bet she'll be glad to lead, or help someone else to lead, a similar project in your area. Let me know what she says."

Before the next meeting, while investigating the problems, team members discovered several things the company obviously was doing wrong. Three of those problems could be eliminated by a simple decision to change the process slightly, so they made the changes, without waiting. One example was entering the effective date of new prices in the computer so that the date of the customer's order automatically determined which price list was to be used.

Third Meeting
The agenda for the third meeting was:

- Review new data
- Discuss reports on studies of problems
- Review revised flow chart
- Imagineer perfect process
- Identify differences between perfect process and present one
- Decide on changes that can be made immediately
- Assign other possible changes for further study

The new data confirmed the original Pareto chart. It also showed that small customers had relatively more errors than large customers. For small customers the major cause of pricing errors was outdated price lists. Bill from Sales volunteered to see what could be done to insure all customers had current price lists.

For large customers, wrong product codes were still the largest single cause of pricing errors. The second largest source of errors was from price concessions approved by Sales but not entered in the computer. Mary asked Bill from Sales and Dan from Billing to make a joint study of the problem to determine the causes in detail and report back at the next meeting.

Bill presented a report on the wrong product codes. He felt confident about the reasons for customer errors and said that they were still working on the reasons for sales correspondents' errors.

Dean presented a Pareto chart of the reasons for billing clerks using wrong product codes, and the two major reasons were: 1) keying in the code for the product above or below the correct one on their list, and 2) transposing numbers during the keying process. They discussed ways of solving those problems and felt that the first one could be largely eliminated by reprinting the list of codes with more space between each item. They also decided to suggest that billing clerks use a ruler to guide their eye in picking out the code.

The second problem could be solved by entering each number twice to verify it, but that would require extra time. After some discussion, Mary agreed to talk to the Information Systems Manager to see if the code numbers could be redesigned with a check digit so a transposed number would trigger an automatic rejection.

Next, Mary presented her revised flow chart and said that she wanted to use that as a basis for imagineering a perfect process. They outlined each step in detail and came up with what they thought would be a foolproof process which would also save considerable time. Dan then drew a flow chart of the "perfect" process on a easel and made sure everyone understood the chart and agreed that it represented the best possible process.

Then the group listed the areas of difference between the present process and the ideal process. This highlighted several additional areas for study.

From the reports on problems at the beginning of the meeting, and from the imagineering study, the group identified several changes that could be made immediately. The remaining problems were assigned for further study and/or preparation of recommendations for solution.

Over the next week group members implemented many improvements and developed solutions for other problems. At the end of the **fourth meeting** they felt the project was almost complete. They set up a system to continue to monitor pricing errors, and Bill promised that Sales would continue to work on their end of the project until they had virtually eliminated the errors.

Everyone felt very good about what they had accomplished. They had eliminated a source of customer irritation, saved the company money by eliminating underbilling errors, and made their own jobs easier.

They were enthusiastic about how they had worked together and decided they should continue the team with a new objective—"Eliminate all errors in billing and shipping paperwork." Mary asked them to think about whether that was the right objective and about what data they would need to attack the problem.

They decided it was time to assign just one person to follow the loose ends on the completed project and continue to monitor their performance. That person assumed the responsibility of putting the new procedures in writing and of educating any new employees in the new system. The group agreed on measurements to check if the process continued to operate as they intended. These included measurements of the process itself, such as the average backlog, and of the results, such as number of errors by cause.

Although the work of many project teams may parallel that of the team in this case, teams may meet 10 or 40 times—rather than 4—before they feel they have accomplished their objective. Team members need to be patient but not too patient—progress may come slowly, and sometimes the largest, most important changes result only after months or, in rare instances, years of work. In order for teams to be successful, you always need leadership, drive, urgency and enthusiasm or not much will happen.

TYPES OF PROJECTS

Since errors are a form of waste, this project was a typical one for finding, quantifying and eliminating the waste. Other projects can be much more complex, but they can then be divided into sub-projects until a relatively small team can handle each sub-project. Senior management coordinates these more complex projects, keeps them on track and allocates resources, creating management-directed programs.

To give you some ideas of typical projects, I will list some under the four categories of material, capital, time, and lost opportunities. Obviously many projects will attack more than one kind of waste. For example, eliminating rework can save material, time, and capital. If the rework is a bottleneck operation, it can also represent lost opportunities.

Attacking Waste of Material

1. Review supplier specifications to see if they are too tight, too loose, or not clearly defined.
2. Establish a partnership with your supplier(s) so that you are both trying to reach the same objectives of low cost and high quality. Work together and share cost reductions. Improve the ordering system by having orders entered electronically from the supplier's computer to yours. Also share information on inventory control, stocking levels, etc.
3. Review specifications with your customer(s) to see if changes can be made that will benefit both parties by lowering cost and/or improving performance.
4. Review vendors' quality performance and work with them to improve. Or find vendors already committed to continuous improvement.
5. Increase yield of good product coming from a manufacturing operation. Identify and quantify causes of scrap

and rework. Set priorities for improvement.

6. Reduce use of supplies by recycling, better measurement and control, etc.

7. Compare material input to a process with material output from the process to discover sources of loss.

8. Study energy use to identify and quantify waste. Analyze lighting, heating, air conditioning, use of process heat and electricity, etc.

9. Study packaging materials to minimize cost, optimize function, and sell more product

10. Analyze inventory losses and controls to reduce shrinkage. Identify sources of losses, prioritize and eliminate them.

11. Review use of forms to see if each is necessary and if all copies are necessary. (Also saves time.)

12. Study the distribution system including suppliers, production facilities and warehouses. Imagineer the perfect distribution system and make plans to get closer to perfection.

13. Review the engineering design process to insure it includes input from manufacturing, purchasing and marketing people.

Attacking Waste of Capital

1. Analyze how to eliminate a bottleneck operation without buying new equipment. Study operating speed, downtime, scheduling, etc.

2. Investigate the various pools of inventory to see if a "Just-in-time" approach can reduce the amount needed.

3. Examine the range of products or services sold to see if the variety offered can be reduced.

4. Review all old (more than three or six months?) inventory and develop a plan to get rid of it. Also plan so that no more inventory becomes "old."

5. Maximize use of present equipment before buying addi-

tional units. Review subcontracting as an alternative to adding equipment.
6. Investigate the feasibility of sharing facilities with another organization. This is particularly important for hospitals requiring very expensive equipment.
7. Find out why customers are not paying their bills on time. Eliminate those reasons.
8. Establish supplier partnerships to develop a seamless process to minimize waste and meet customer needs. Cooperate on design. Reduce or eliminate bidding and minimize other costs.

Attacking Waste of Time

This is the most important area to study, since most waste comes from the things we work on and the way we work. A lot of waste goes unrecognized because people don't make a methodical study of the way time is spent. This is particularly true for non-manufacturing areas. A disciplined method of determining how time is spent and what activities are performed will identify the waste and thus help you eliminate it. This methodology is covered in detail in this book.

Projects to discover waste of time usually use one or more of the following techniques.
1. Review how time of machines or people is being spent. Identify what is being done that does not add value or is of low value. Increase value added work by at least 50%.
2. Study scheduling of work and personnel and try to insure that people have full-time value-added work available to do at all times.
3. Study processes and methods by which work is being done to discover and make improvements.
4. Imagineer the perfect way to accomplish the work in the least time.
5. Identify key areas of work such as the design, development, manufacture and sale of a new product or service.

Measure current performance in time. Study, change and improve appropriate processes to reduce total time.

Attacking Waste Caused by Lost Opportunities

1. Study your process for developing new products and/or services.

   Review the following:
   - The time it takes to get new products to market
   - Your system for discovering customer needs
   - Competitors' performance in introducing new products

   Then imagineer what your process for new products should be.

2. Review your market share by area. What are the "good" areas and the "bad" areas? What lessons can you learn from each type to improve your overall share?

3. Study why you lose orders. Institute a "lost order report" for sales people. See whether your delivery times are competitive.

4. Investigate what new technologies might be used in your operations. What new developments may have application? What are your competitors doing? What is happening in other markets/countries?

5. Study what partnerships (research, marketing, production, outsourcing, etc.) with other organizations would be mutually beneficial.

6. If you have capacity problems that restrict sales, start a project to eliminate bottlenecks.

7. How do sales and marketing people spend their time? Get rid of the waste of time so they can sell more.

CHAPTER 6
MAJOR MANAGEMENT
INNOVATIONS

Almost all major improvement projects require study and innovation by management; therefore I call them Major Management Innovations (MMI). In addition to major projects to improve effectiveness, efficiency and quality, these include major restructuring and evaluations of the basic direction of the organization— such things as changes in product line, marketing strategy, and new product development strategy. This type of project is often called reengineering. The business world is flocking to reengineering and business publications are awash in articles about it. This has reduced effort on continuous improvement because many people believe that reengineering replaces continuous improvement. Actually, reengineering is part of continuous improvement and it always has been.

Reengineering (MMI) is not new. It has been going on continuously throughout the 19th and 20th centuries. Major changes in work processes take place as management innovates and technology changes.

Ford reengineered the auto industry with the mass production of the Model T.

General Motors (under Sloan) did it again.

Toyota did it again.

It will be done again. Entrepreneurs do it all the time.

MMI allows a new company to be successful in an existing market.

It enables divisions of large companies to be successful when they are spun off on their own.

It helps an organization make a major advance in competitive position.

What is reengineering? Hammer and Champy in their book, *Reengineering the Corporation,* define it as: "The fundamental rethinking and radical redesign of business processes to achieve dramatic improvements in critical, contemporary measures of performance, such as cost, quality, service and speed." The opportunities for reengineering are huge. These opportunities naturally evolve from the process of identifying, quantifying and eliminating waste.

Major change will take place, however, only with sufficient management imperative. Most people find it difficult to take the initiative to make drastic changes that affect their jobs. Department managers and others may resist major changes and may even complain that major process changes undermine people's willingness to work on continuous improvement. The key lies in proper and timely education of the people, effective, well-publicized work to create new jobs with new products and services and/or increased market share, and well thought-out plans to take care of people. The way to treat people is discussed in more detail at the end of this chapter and in Chapter 8.

Continuous improvement is necessary at all levels of the organization. The organizational pyramid shows two types of continuous improvement projects: the type done at all levels which anyone can lead, and the type which must be led by the management of the organization. For these major projects management must provide the innovation, the commitment and the resources.

Continuous Improvement

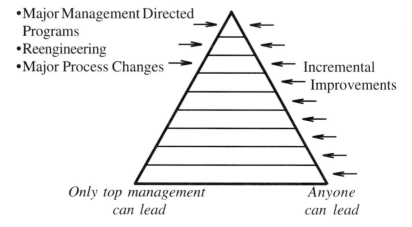

•Major Management Directed
  Programs
•Reengineering
•Major Process Changes   Incremental
                                          Improvements

*Only top management   Anyone
       can lead   can lead*

OTHER PROJECT LEVELS

In addition to projects which are major management innovations (level one) there are projects at three other levels.

Level two—Large projects involving two or more departments or functions (cross-functional).

Level three—Projects contained within one department using, primarily, its own resources.

Level four—Individual projects that people can accomplish largely on their own.

Many of these projects at lower levels are generated to support an MMI project. They can, however, be completely independent of an MMI and be initiated at any level.

In a hospital, the four kinds of projects might include:

Level one—Major management innovations—Analyze and improve work of nurses, aides and hospital administration to improve quality of care and increase productivity at least 20%. Develop flow charts for treatments of all standard diagnoses. Study and improve each treatment process so that the average hospital stay is reduced by at least 30%.

Level two—interdepartmental project—Increase X-ray capacity by over 50% without additional equipment through a combination of better scheduling, changed and improved work processes, and extended hours.

Level three—departmental project—Assure no obstetrics patient waits longer than 60 seconds for response to nurse call button.

Level four—individual project (for a respiratory therapist)— Coordinate services so that none of my patients who are discharged, needing continuing oxygen, arrives home before oxygen set-up is delivered.

Four examples for a bank are:

Level one—Develop and market new financial products for
the bank so that in five years 30% of revenue and profits
will come from new products and services.

Level two—Through scheduling, training, queue management, and perhaps new technology, equipment, or software, insure no customer waits longer than four minutes in
a teller queue, and that the average wait is under two
minutes.

Level three—Reduce the average time for processing a
mortgage application by at least two days.

Level four (for a teller)—Develop a list of value-added
activities I can pursue when no customer is waiting.

Almost all the projects are customer-oriented and will also
reduce costs through eliminating waste. The mind set is continuous
improvement in the organization's ability to please customers
effectively and efficiently.

IDENTIFYING MMI OPPORTUNITIES

How do you decide when a major management innovation is
needed? Review the following list of symptoms of waste.
- High inventories
- High customer complaints, returns and allowances
- High levels of rework
- Long cycle times
- Poor on-time delivery performance
- Long product development cycles
- Poor communications and transitions between R&D,
  Engineering, and Manufacturing
- Heavily layered organizations
- High levels of non-value-added work
- Poor process yields

- Declining market share
- Businesses that would like to relocate to low labor states or countries as a solution to problems
- Quality based on high levels of inspection
- Complex product mix with many similar yet discrete products
- Poor safety record
- Poor environmental compliance
- Low organizational esteem and morale
- Lack of teamwork throughout the organization
- High levels of expediting to make things happen

There are companies, currently very successful and leaders in their industries, that have most of the problems listed above, but don't know it yet! They are the General Motors and Fords of the 1960's and early 1970's or the IBMs and Digitals of the 1970's and early 1980's. They were full of waste but isolation, arrogance, and self-satisfaction prevented them from seeing it. They are doomed to repeat the mistakes of G.M., Ford, IBM and Digital. They need MMI!

Then there are the truly great companies—Toyota, Motorola, Xerox, Dow and others. They continually improve through both incremental improvement and major management led innovation. They ensure success and growth by improving all phases of their operations faster than the competition. They know that there is always substantial waste even in the best systems. Large systems, collections of processes, are often the focus of MMI. Toyota's order placement to cash collection is a huge system. Its continuous improvement is also central to their success.

Our Mail Order Photo Finishing example applied MMI to the entire business system from marketing to the consumer receiving a finished order in the mail. This MMI included the US Mail system!

A similar effort was shown in a Computer Products Division of a large NYSE company. This effort took coated computer disk yields from the industry average of 65% to 95%. This same effort was applied to other major processes and transformed the business to world class in less than two years.

Another way to identify MMI opportunities is to ask the following questions:

What would corporate raiders do if they acquired your company/division?

For a division of a larger company—What would you do if you were spun off to shareholders in a separate company?

For someone whose market share is 15% or lower—Why don't you have double your current market share?

For someone who is # 1 in the market—Why don't you have 10% more market share?

The truth is that all companies must do MMI. It is a major responsibility of management and long term survival is at stake.

Management should also consider the effects of any MMI on people. Major management innovations, like any other part of continuous improvement, should help people and treat them with respect. Employment security is on everyone's mind. Providing such security should be a top priority of every organization.

For the great majority of incremental improvements, employment security is not a substantial issue. Examples include:

- Part of a job eliminated due to reduction in rework.
- A reduction in inventory or accounts receivable.
- Product and service improvements to increase sales and customer satisfaction.
- Modest improvements in yields in a manufacturing industry over 1 to 2 years.
- Modest improvements of administrative or service activities over time.

Management should make clear that many major management innovations do not affect employment security. Examples include:

- Major reductions in material costs through use of alternate materials and/or redesign.
- Major reductions in inventory (50 days to 10 days) or receivables (60 days to 30 days).
- Major product improvements to increase sales and improve customer satisfaction.
- Major new products or services.

In some cases, however, human relations can be a more difficult problem. Examples include:

- Doubling the productivity of a process where hundreds of people work.
- Completely revamping the engineering design process to make it more productive.
- Substantially changing the computer systems to automate many administrative and financial jobs.
- Eliminating rework in a major process by doing things right the first time.

In such cases, it is quickly clear to everyone that there is a substantial potential employment security problem. In such cases, treat people as you would like to be treated. Some key items are:

- Educate people in continuous improvement so they understand what it is and why it is necessary.
- Do whatever is practical to create new productive jobs to take care of people.
- Shut the front door to new hires except for a few specialists.
- Use attrition whenever possible.
- Use MMI on a rolling and regular basis for various business units. Make it part of the way you regularly do business so that everyone is familiar with it.
- Develop a well thought out and generous (based on

company conditions) program to take care of people, including golden handshakes, helping people get new jobs, providing training, counseling, etc.

- When we have to reduce substantially the number of people for survival and growth of the business, follow these above key items but do it quickly. Get it over and put it behind you—the sooner the better.
- Always remember that these major reductions often come from organizations with a history of not studying, changing and improving the work. The more frequently we make the changes the easier it is to do them and take care of the people.

CHAPTER 7
ANALYZE WORK AND ELIMINATE WASTE

Whether you're looking for waste of material, capital, time, or lost opportunities, to find the waste, study and analyze the <u>work</u> and <u>work processes</u>. Waste derives from work—what you choose to work on and how you work. It includes the work of machines, computers, chemical processes and people. Most people cannot tell you, in any detailed manner, how they spend their time at work. Furthermore, few examine their activities to see which of those activities add value from the customers' viewpoint. Most of the waste usually comes from working on the wrong things, things that have become part of the work process but don't really add value for the customer. Therefore, everyone needs to perform a detailed analysis of the work being done, including an evaluation of what the customer wants. The work of people leads directly to all other work—like that of machines, computers, and chemical processes. An organization can and should analyze ALL forms of work. Major management innovations often come from customer requirements, low profitability, new technologies, changed markets or competitive analysis. People, including senior management, see opportunity for major changes and improvements.

CRUCIAL CONCEPTS FOR FINDING THE WASTE

As you begin to find the waste, you should be able to:

- understand, in great detail, what work is being done and why.
- determine which work has value or is necessary, and eliminate all other work.
- eliminate the waste in the remaining work using ideas from all levels of the organization.

- use some simple tools to gather and classify data about the work being done, including the cost and value of the work.
- look for new ways to do value added and necessary work better and quicker. Use imagineering and creative questioning to examine the work.
- involve everyone and keep them fully informed.
- search external customer needs, technology and equipment changes for new value added work.

THE MAIN EVENT

The "main event" in continuous improvement is the elimination of waste by improving and changing the processes of work, using the concepts just listed and the simple tools described in the next section. The following diagram extracts the "main event" from the model of continuous improvement.

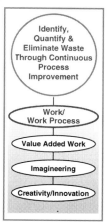

Finding and eliminating waste through continuous process improvement is the main event because it is the key to continuous improvement. This is the activity that:

- reduces costs
- improves quality

- uncovers opportunities
- makes you more competitive.

The system is so powerful because it allows you to accomplish these four things by focusing on one activity, the core activity of identifying, quantifying and eliminating waste. Every problem is an opportunity. By searching for the waste and finding the problems causing the waste, you create opportunities to solve the problems, change and/or improve the processes, and eliminate the waste. Failure to take advantage of opportunities to do things like increase sales and develop new products is often the largest waste. Include these added opportunities in the search for waste.

Some people are surprised that eliminating waste not only reduces costs, but improves quality at the same time. This is the "Quality Secret." Quality problems can be traced to some characteristic of the product or service. Problems are caused by that characteristic being at the wrong level or varying too much. The chart below shows how one product was improved by changing the level of one of its characteristics and reducing the variation.

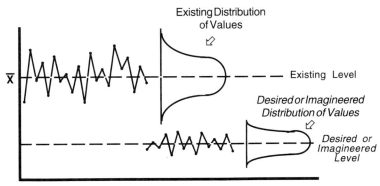

The wrong level and/or excess variation are forms of waste. For example, if the thickness of a coating on a sheet of carbonless paper is too high, this causes waste of coating material. If it is too low, it will make an inadequate copy and be rejected as waste.

Additional waste is caused by excessive variation in the coating thickness. By constantly searching out the causes for waste, you can reduce the variation in your processes, improve the level and achieve higher and higher quality at lower and lower cost. Some companies using continuous improvement techniques have reduced defectives from parts per hundred to a few parts per million, or even per billion, while reducing costs at the same time.

This success results from everyone focusing on the core activity of finding, quantifying and eliminating the waste. People working in all phases of a process are the best ones to identify waste in each of their areas including customer satisfaction, the time activities take, the quality of a service or product, cost, productivity or sales of a product or service.

Studying Waste at "Macro" and "Micro" Levels

Waste needs to be studied at two levels, the "macro" level and the "micro" or "detailed" level. The macro level includes major changes in technology, equipment, methods or processes. (See Chapter 4.) Looking for micro waste means examining the details of all the work processes to find all the waste—that work which does not add value to the customer. Initial progress often comes through many, many small improvements. But the purpose of the initial studies will be to find out what work is being done and classify it in categories to enable you to find and eliminate the waste. Over time, this succession of small changes frequently leads to massive overall improvement.

At the same time each person should consider major "macro" changes in the way he or she works. A change is "macro" or "detailed" only in relation to the person, level and area of the organization involved. To a process operator, starting to use a computer terminal to enter and retrieve information may be a major change, but to the chief executive, it is micro. The chief executive considers macro changes to be such things as changes in product line, marketing channels, technology, financial structure, motivation of people, number of people, or manufacturing technology.   Although most of the following discussion concentrates on micro waste, macro waste—the big questions, issues, and decisions over which top management has control—accounts for at least half of the potential gains in any organization.

Project Work and Identification of Waste

Identifying and quantifying waste will often lead to eliminating that waste without formal project work.   Once you identify problems and break them down into small enough pieces it can become obvious what to do to eliminate waste and improve the process.   For example, you may discover that you are doing something no longer needed. Perhaps you are preparing a monthly report that was important at one time but is no longer used. In that case a decision to eliminate the report would eliminate some wasted work.   Or you may find that a substantial amount of administrative or manufacturing waste is caused by failure to train new operators. Again the solution is an obvious one.

Often, however, you need a project to identify the waste. Consider a complex process with an unsatisfactorily low yield of good product. A project will be necessary to discover all the reasons for low yield and to develop ways to eliminate those problems. Similarly, reducing customer complaints may require a project to identify the reasons for those complaints in enough detail so that corrective action can be taken. Project work and waste identification are closely intertwined. Even when the solution is obvious, it usually takes some work to eliminate that waste.

TOOLS

Along with a knowledge of the forms of waste and the ways of looking for waste, several tools are particularly helpful for identifying and setting priorities for projects. The best tools for finding the waste are:

Assessment of the Current Situation

The current assessment of the overall organization was discussed on pages 88-92. People at all levels should help to assess their own work and that of their department or other work unit. An individual assessment includes:

- Human relations factors (Chapter 8). How do I communicate with others and do I treat them with respect?
- Looking for "macro" waste. What is "macro" depends on the job of the person. Ask yourself the following:
  - Do I have the right tools for the job?
  - Do I have the necessary skills and training for the job?
  - Is necessary information available to me?
  - Is my work organized properly?
  - Is my work scheduled properly?
  - Are my priorities established?
  - Do I have good relationships with suppliers to the work process?
  - Do I have good relationships with customers of the work process?

Add any pertinent questions of your own to the list. Just thinking through this list and then making an assessment of each of the factors often brings wasteful practices to light. For example, people may discover waste caused by not understanding customer needs, by not planning their work, or by not having the right tools.

Talking to (surveying) fellow employees, suppliers and customers about the work process is a good way to discover things that need improvement. It is also a good way of discovering things you and others are doing that do not add value.

At the supervisory or managerial level, ask the same type of questions about the whole work unit.

Flow charting is a powerful but simple tool that helps you document and understand what work is being done. It can be applied to the design of a nuclear submarine, to making a budget, or to cashing a check. It can also clearly show the opportunities for improvement.

Work analysis is a system for describing and classifying the work in an organized fashion. Just finding out and documenting what is being done and how long it takes will uncover many areas of waste.

Work sampling helps you determine how much time is being spent on each activity.

Costing the activities and tasks enables you to compare the cost of each with its value to your customers. This approach differs from normal cost accounting. It is also called "activity based costing." Many organizations look at activity based costing as a separate activity from Continuous Improvement. It really is another very important tool for evaluating work in continuous improvement. How much do the various activities cost? Bob Kaplan of Harvard University who initiated "Activity Based Costing" now often calls his work "Activity Based Management".

Questioning activities and tasks in a disciplined fashion is a powerful tool for rooting out waste.

Looking for bottlenecks is a key way to make major improvements in capacity or time to do things.

Methods analysis is a structured way of looking at the present process and questioning the way it is being done. Most methods improvements are the result of studying the present process and using innovation, creativity, accumulated knowledge and constant drive for improvement to improve the way things are being done. Work sampling and flow charts are very good ways of studying the present process.

The Six Questions of Methods Analysis
Analyze any process by asking six important questions:

1. **"Do we need to do this work at all?"** There's no point in improving a process that isn't necessary.
2. **"Can we eliminate steps?"** Can movement of material or paperwork be eliminated? Can inspection or checking steps be eliminated? Can this particular segment of work be cut completely?
3. **"Should we change the process?"** If a segment of work cannot be eliminated completely, can it be fundamentally changed to reduce the time involved? Remember, time is your raw material. Can the technology be changed? Can it be done more effectively by someone else, at some other time, in some other manner? Should some of the steps in the process be changed?
4. **"Should we combine steps?"** How can two things that you do at the same time be combined? Or three things? Can part of the work be combined with an operation in a previous or subsequent department?
5. **"Should we rearrange steps?"** Can you rearrange the work? Will it be more efficient if you re-order the steps in the process?
6. **"Can we simplify the work?"** Most people start out with this question, when, in fact, it should be the last. Simplifying work that should be eliminated is not true work improvement. When, however, the first five questions have been asked and used to improve the work, the last step to consider is how to simplify what is left.

View time as a raw material and focus on value-added work. And ask yourself the above six questions—can the work (or individual steps) be eliminated, changed, combined, rearranged, or simplified? Look at the time used to perform value-added work, and see how even that work can be eliminated, changed, combined, rearranged, or simplified to make it more effective.

Imagineering can be used with work analysis, methods analysis, or assessment of the current situation. Any time you determine how things *are*, use imagineering to ponder *how they might be*. This tool, probably the most powerful one of all, is particularly effective for use in group discussions. By imagining the way things could or should be, you get an idea of the potential for improvement. Imagineering helps people approach the problem with no preconceived notions of what should be done or how it should be done. While methods analysis helps you make continuing improvements in the process, imagineering often helps to make real breakthroughs in improving or eliminating work for people, machines, computers and processes. Imagineering creates the delta, the difference, between the way things are and the way they could or should be. It is that difference which releases creativity and innovation of our people.

In Appendix A we will explain how to use these tools in a disciplined approach to analyzing work, finding the waste, and getting rid of it. This analysis can be done at all levels of the organization. The "vital few" major programs of the organization and the everyday work processes all need to be analyzed. Top managers make the most important decisions about work—What countries should we do business in? What new product lines or business should we enter? But front-line supervisors or department managers usually lead the analysis of the work of most of the organization's people. Therefore, the following material will be discussed from the point of view of a unit supervisor, although it can be applied, with some modification, to work processes at all levels.

Remember that all improvements—Major Management Innovations or small incremental improvements—come down to knowledge of the work. If we are making a major process change we still have to get down to the details of the new work after the change. We should try to get most of the waste out of that work right up front. We can only do that if we have people at all levels who know how important it is and who will lead this change.

CHAPTER 8
RESPECT PEOPLE

People working in teams, motivated through joy in achievement to make continuous improvement, are a very powerful force in an organization. They are the heart of the continuous improvement system. Effective teams can be successfully created only with sufficient training. To help bring about the culture change and resulting behavioral changes required for success, human relations practices need to:

- Foster an atmosphere of teamwork, where people work together toward common goals and share their knowledge with others
- Treat everyone fairly
- Value the contribution of each person
- Provide leaders that coach, help, enable, empower and trust, rather than direct and judge
- Show people that it is in their self-interest to adopt continuous improvement, since it will pay off for them in increased motivation, joy in achievement, and team interaction. It also makes their organization more competitive, therefore increasing their employment security.

HUMAN RELATIONS PROCESS CHECKS

Review these five questions to process check your human relations activities.

1. The Golden Rule
Do you treat people as you would like to be treated?
Respect for people in continuous improvement means more than just treating people with respect and with consideration for their feelings. It means showing respect for their brain power, wanting their participation and asking for their suggestions. The

people who know the most about the troubles, problems, lost opportunities and waste in any work process are the people doing the work. However, they are working within a system established by management, and usually only management has the power to change the system. In the traditional system, management tells people what to do and then judges how well they perform. The people are not asked or expected to make changes to improve the work process. Consequently traditional organizations ignore their major source of knowledge about waste.

Another reason people working in the system do not help discover waste is that they are afraid that they will be blamed for the waste or that their boss will be angry because they are being critical of management. Overcome this feeling by assuring and demonstrating that everyone receives amnesty.

In this new system, people learn to look for waste, for problems, and bring them out into the open rather than hide them. To encourage this, show by actions that you are not interested in laying blame, but only in identifying the waste so that it can be eliminated. When people understand that at least 85% of the problems are the fault of the system rather than the individual, and that they will be given amnesty for their past mistakes, they will be forthcoming.

In continuous improvement, managers and the people work-ing with them act as a team, in an atmosphere of mutual trust. The manager, acting as player/coach, empowers the team members to suggest and make improvements in the work process. Manage-ment creates an atmosphere in which working on continuous improvement is the accepted manner of day-to-day operation. People whose ideas are wanted and respected feel much better about their jobs than people who are told just to do the job and not "make waves." Respect for their ideas about how to do the work greatly increases people's self-respect and job satisfaction. When working groups feel that management wants their ideas and values them as part of a team, they often change their attitude from indifference to their work and antagonism toward management to active cooperation, with absenteeism dropping dramatically and with huge increases in productivity.

For people to work in continuous improvement, they have to be convinced they will be treated fairly. To many, "treated fairly" means being given secure employment or seeing the organization use its best efforts to provide secure employment and helping them when it cannot do so.

Case: Layoffs to Come

In Nashua's Computer Products Division in 1981, we had made huge yield improvements in our major product line of computer memory disks—from an average of 65% to 95% in only 9 months. This improvement and others also increased quality and productivity dramatically. Approximately 100 people were employed directly in making those disks. While our business was expanding, we were not able to increase the business fast enough to keep everyone productively employed.

Early in August the Vice President of Personnel, dropped into my office to tell me about the Computer Products Division. He said, "We have been doing all that great work up there and making those tremendous improvements. Well, the General Manager, was in to see me a couple of days ago, and said they have about 40 too many people up there. As you know, our General Managers have the right to hire and fire within certain guidelines and he is telling us we really need a lay-off of about 40 people. We have been looking around, and we can find a place for 20 of the people in other Divisions that need people, but we will never be able to do it for 40 people. And, Bill, you know what that is going to mean. People are going to see that they worked for continuous improvement and their reward for that is that they get laid off. I just wanted you to know what would be happening in a few days."

We talked about the problem and I said, "Well, I guess we don't want to change the rules at this time regarding the rights of General Managers in lay-offs. However, why don't you go see the General Manager and tell him we have been over this thing about the lay-off of 20 people, and he will have to comply with a couple of new practices.

"Number one: all lay-offs of people for downsizing will be made consistent with the ratio of salaried to hourly people in the Division. In this case, we have a need for 20 fewer people. We have 225 hourly people and about 225 salaried people in that business, so we will divide that 20 into 10 salaried and 10 hourly. He can lay off any 10 salaried people he wants along with the 10 hourly people, but that's the way we'll do it.

"Number two: lay-offs are a serious corporate event and no longer is some low level person from human resources going to handle the lay-off along with the first level supervisor from the area concerned. No one can be terminated or laid off without having a full briefing with the senior management. The General Manager and the other top people—Sales and Marketing, R&D, Engineering, Manufacturing, Administration, Controller—need to meet with all 450 people in the next 48 hours. They need to explain what is going on in the business, what they are trying to do about getting more business, and why this lay-off is necessary now. They should allow themselves plenty of time, with reasonably small groups—no more than 25 people. After they give them the briefing they are going to expose themselves for up to one hour of questions by the people as to what is really going on. And I mean all the people, third shift, everyone."

The VP of Personnel said, "That's going to take some time and hard work, night and day."

I said, "That's right. Working in the new system is not easy. We have to face up to the reality of the situation and take care of the people."

So he did it. You can imagine what happened at those meetings. Someone came in to see me first thing Monday morning to tell me about the meeting on the third shift. Many meetings had already been held, so everyone knew what was coming and that everyone was going to have a chance to ask their questions.

The first question for the Sales Manager went something like

this: "Len, we used to have a lot of business here in those black and orange boxes, but we haven't had any for a few months. Which company had those black and orange boxes anyway?"

Mgr: "Oh, XYZ Company."
Staff: "We don't do business with them anymore?"
Mgr: "Well, not in that big item, we don't do any business."
Staff: "Oh? Tell me, what percent of the sales was that?"
Mgr: "About 2% of total sales."
Staff: "What percent of the physical volume—they were manufacturing drives weren't they?
Mgr: "Yes, it was almost 4%."

The staff person quickly calculated that 4% of 450 people was 18 people whose jobs were lost when the company lost that customer. Further questioning revealed that the manager had visited the customer only once, six months before it stopped placing orders. The staff person's last question was, "It wasn't that important to you?"

Another question was addressed to the Head of the R&D Group.

Staff: "I remember back in June when we had that trial, they told us how important it was so we'd all cooperate in every way to make it successful. They said we expected to obtain an increase in overall business of approximately 10% by the end of the year. They said how urgent it was. We had troubles in the trial. Some of the formulae didn't seem to work the way we expected. The trial was less successful than people wanted. That was in June and here it is more than two months later, and we haven't heard another thing. Now 10%—that would be another 40-45 jobs. Even on a marginal basis it would be at least 30 jobs. Tell me, all those R&D people and those Engineering

people that are working on this, are they all working 7 days a week, 8, 10, 12 hours a day, trying to get that ready so all the rest of us will have jobs?"

I talked with the General Manager, a couple of days later and he told me he now understood what continuous improvement was all about when it came to human relations and treating people as you would want to be treated if you were in their position. He now understood that it meant that all of us should be doing everything we could at all times to take care of our people, including getting new business and doing everything else to maintain our competitive edge.

The General Manager deferred most lay offs and went to work on increasing the business more rapidly. New sales came from an entirely new level of understanding of the need for action and motivation by the senior management of the business. Every manager and supervisor understood this new responsibility. The R&D and Sales departments had an entirely new idea of their responsibility in helping to provide more business and to create more jobs. Word spread like wildfire through the company. Now human relations was real and tangible. Managers did care about the people!

2. The System is the Problem
Are your actions consistent with the fact that 90% or more of all the troubles, waste and opportunities for improvement come from the process or the system, and not the individual?

Case: Tracking Down the Handling Damage
In a company making photoconductive drums for copying machines, handling damage to the product during processing caused great concern, since it led to twenty per cent of all rejections. The superintendent met with the process operators, criticized them for their carelessness, and told them they might lose

business if their costs due to damage did not come down. Several such meetings produced no significant change in handling damage. Next the superintendent made a study and identified the amount of handling damage caused by each operator. He posted the results weekly on a bulletin board. Soon people began to joke about who would get the "Clumsy Award" for the week. Still the handling damage continued at about the same rate. This went on for over a year and continued as a source of conflict between the operators and supervisors.

Meanwhile, the corporation began the process of continuous improvement. The superintendent attended a seminar during which he learned that 90-95% of the problems come from the process itself, not the process operators. Further, he learned that the workers were the "experts" who knew more about the troubles and problems in a process than anyone else.

Although he didn't really believe what he had been told, he decided to try a different approach. He held a meeting with the operators and told them what he had learned at the seminar. He admitted the possibility that he had been using the wrong approach to handling damage. He acknowledged that they probably knew much more about the process than he did. He then asked for their help. He asked them to think about all the problems in the process that might cause handling damage, and he asked for their suggestions for changes. He scheduled another meeting for a week later.

He couldn't believe the number of good suggestions that came from that meeting. One was:

> The drums were held vertically on the conveyor belt at a fairly high level. This made them difficult to grasp securely when removing them, particularly for short operators. The obvious solution was to lower the conveyor belt and position them horizontally.

> Another one was: Storage racks, which held six drums each, allowed very little space between the drums, making

it difficult to insert or remove drums without causing a scratch. Solution? Increase the spacing and/or change the process so that interim storage was not necessary.

The operators provided seven other good suggestions for reducing handling damage. The superintendent was amazed. He was now convinced that almost all the problems were the fault of the process, but he had never asked the operators because he hadn't respected their knowledge or brain power.

Toward the end of the meeting, one of the operators asked, "Will you take a suggestion on something other than handling damage?"

"Sure," he replied.

"You know our reclaim operation, where we remove the coating from rejected drums so that the aluminum tube can be reused? I've been making little marks on the end of reclaimed tubes so I could see if they come back through the reclaim line again. You know that cleaning tank, where we change the cleaning solution over every weekend? I've noticed that the tubes that get reclaimed on Monday or Tuesday don't come back to reclaim very often. But it gets worse as the week goes on, and I'd say by Friday, at least 50% of the reclaimed drums get rejected and come back to reclaim again. Maybe by Friday that cleaning solution is too dirty or too weak to do the job anymore."

The superintendent was amazed. Why hadn't the engineers discovered that? He commended the operator for her suggestion and asked if they could meet again the next week for suggestions from any area. He said he would make an industrial engineer available to them full-time for the week to help them gather data and answer any questions they might have about the process.

Over the next two months, handling damage went down by 90%. Over the next year rejections from all causes dropped by 73%. The attitude of the operators and superintendent changed dramatically. They all felt part of a team that was achieving exciting things and making the company more competitive. The operators liked coming to work, and absenteeism dropped by half. They felt that the process was theirs and their ideas were treated with respect. The "Clumsy Award" was replaced by the "Idea of the Month." It was often awarded to a team or group.

3. Cooperate, Don't Compete

Do people believe it is in their interest to share their knowledge of the best way to work, to cooperate rather than compete?

Human relations systems in most organizations concentrate on the individual. The measurement and rewards systems are designed to measure individuals and to reward or punish individuals. Organizations educate, train and motivate individuals. Praising and rewarding the best performers and penalizing the not-so-good performers encourages people to compete with each other rather than cooperate. In continuous improvement we want to raise the whole group or team performance, moving away from heavy dependence on individual performance to new systems more dependent on team performance. Individuals still receive recognition, but that recognition is for their contribution to the group and its efforts.

The primary person to make this change is the supervisor or manager. The leader's praise sends a signal as to what performance the organization desires. If the leader praises behavior that contributes to improvement of the whole team, then people will work for the team. If, on the other hand, people are judged individually and competitively, they will do what is necessary to enhance their individual performance in comparison with others. They will avoid sharing their knowledge with others and/or teaching their skills to others.

Case: The Lone Star Becomes a Team Player

A design engineering group spent most of its time developing drawings of items to be fabricated in a machine shop. They used computers with the latest computer aided design software. One of the design engineers named Andy was a star performer. He produced nearly twice as many drawings as the average engineer in the group and almost never made an error. The head design engineer gave all the critical jobs to Andy, constantly praised him, and used his work as a benchmark to exhort the others to do better work. When free tickets to sporting events became available, Andy always got them. Andy had a cheerful personality, but he was secretive about his work. He never liked anyone to watch him when he was preparing a drawing. The other group members resented him and did not socialize with him. After Andy's company had been involved with continuous improvement for about six months, the boss called him in for a talk. He said something like this.

"Andy, I'm afraid I haven't done as good a job of managing this group as you have done with your design work."

Andy replied, "What do you mean? Have I been doing something wrong?"

"No, I have. We are going to get some substantial new orders and we are going to have to improve the productivity of the whole design team. The way I have been managing has encouraged each person to do his or her best. You have done extremely well and continue to improve even more. But this hasn't brought along the rest of the group. I know that you have some knowledge, some skills, some tricks of the trade that the others don't have. Our job now is to multiply your skills by bringing up the skills of the others closer to your level.

"I need your help to change the way I have been managing. From now on, I want our group to work as a team. My job as coach will be to raise the performance level of the whole team, not just you, my star player. I want you to help me in this coaching job. You can make a much larger contribution to the organization by helping others to do a better job than by just doing an outstanding job in your own work. I want you to start spending half of each day helping the others learn how to do their job better. I know I am asking you to share some of your secrets, but by sharing them, you will gain greater recognition of your skills."

Andy was not so sure that he liked the idea, because it was such a different way of thinking for him. But he respected his boss and promised to give it a try. He soon found that it gave him a great deal of satisfaction to help the others and see them improve. As the new orders began to come in, the productivity of the whole group improved. What's more, Andy was surprised to learn that some of the other engineers had tricks of the trade that could help him do his job better. Whenever someone showed significant improvement, Andy got some of the credit. Most importantly, he began to receive praise from his peers as well as his boss. Andy became accepted as the star member of the team, not just the star.

4. Remove Artificial Caps

Do you have artificial caps on the quality and productivity of the work?

People are often judged by how well they meet their budget, their targets, or their objectives. These objectives are often set either arbitrarily or by negotiation. The assumptions underlying targets or objectives are that a certain level of performance is attainable, that the level is "good" and that people can be motivated to reach that level if the objective is defined for them.

The people trying to reach the objective are naturally concerned about what will happen if they don't reach it. They are also concerned that if the objective is met, it will likely be raised for a subsequent period. Because of the uncertainty of the future, people being judged want to set a low target to be sure they can meet it, even if the most unlikely events occur.

Once a target is set, many people do not like to exceed that target by very much, for fear of raising future expectations and/or being accused of "sandbagging"—withholding relevant information—by setting too low a target. Managers, on the other hand, want a reasonably high target for their subordinates (though not for themselves) so that the target creates the drive to try hard, thus relieving the manager of the responsibility to help motivate others.

Case: "I Don't Want To Know"

A vice-president of a large organization, Karl, was preparing a presentation for the Chief Executive and his staff. He had worked with his Budget Manager, Larry, to prepare the targets in terms of sales, expense savings, requirements for capital, etc. The vice-president knew from past experience that whatever he submitted was likely to be revised to make the targets tougher, so they were discussing each of the targets. He finally said to his Budget Manager, "Larry, you know it's going to be tough getting new people and money for new capital expenditures. I am going to have to go up there, scream and shout and bleed all over the floor so that we don't get cut back too much. Just so I'll know, how much do you think we could really get by with next year if we had to?" Before Larry could answer, he said, "No! Wait! Don't tell me! If I really know how much we need, my performance won't be as convincing. They'll see I really don't need what I'm asking for and cut me back more. If I'm not sure, I'll be more worried and they'll see my concern. Wish me good luck!"

This really happened. Similar things occur at all levels in many organizations. This attitude generates under-performance because people spend so much time and effort protecting themselves from what they believe may be unreasonable targets. Then, once the targets are set, they work to meet them, but not to exceed them by much, to maintain their credibility and flexibility in setting future targets.

Organizations working on continuous improvement eliminate such talk and the thinking behind it; they try not to set limits or end points for how much they can improve. They often set short term goals, but they recognize from the start that they will continue to raise such goals until continuous improvement becomes ingrained in the thinking of everyone in the organization.

In place of the desire for protection that this case highlights, people need to feel a desire for achievement. People working in continuous improvement receive great satisfaction from the improvements they make, and this satisfaction spurs them on to seek additional improvements. They try to achieve the maximum they can without worrying how their achievement will affect some artificial goal-setting in the future.

Goal setting by negotiation is ingrained in Western management style. Business schools teach Management by Objectives (MBO) as a basis for giving people the incentive to perform and judging people's performance the natural result is that people being judged try to negotiate goals they are sure they can meet. Then they avoid exceeding those goals so that next year's new objectives will not be too difficult. For the person approving the objectives it provides an easy way to manage. Set the objectives, look at the results and reward or punish accordingly. This is an abdication of leadership. How much better to have people work as a team trying to achieve the best results possible.

Budgets are necessary for planning, but they are also often negotiated as objectives for sales, costs, expenses, productivity, etc. This leads to less than optimum results. It is not wrong to have goals, but they should be in the form of continuous improvement, such as improve productivity by at least 0.5% a month—forever. Too often something which takes two days to do now, took the same amount of time last year, and five years ago. What we have is another cap on the quality and productivity of the work!

5. Know the Benefits of the New System

Do people in your organization know how the new system benefits them?

The benefits of the continuous improvement system are many for the people working in the system. The most important benefit is that it works in a way that helps everyone. As a result people enjoy:

- More challenging work
- Joy in achievement
- More self respect
- Feeling part of a team

- Pride in a more competitive organization
- Working the new way because it is "right"
- Being able to help others in or out of their organization to improve any kind of work

Working this new way is also the only real employment security, although this is hard for some people to accept.

I know of organizations where people recognized all of these benefits, but after a while they stopped working on continuous improvement because they perceived that further improvement could make fewer people necessary and cost them their jobs. There is no easy way to allay such fears. Of course, the best solution is to use reduced costs and increased quality to get more business, and this can often be done. If it can't be done, people should at least perceive they are being treated fairly.

While no one can guarantee people's jobs in all circumstances, some companies get around this problem by making a commitment similar to the following.

"No one will lose their job because of progress made in the continuous improvement process. As we become more efficient, we will do our best to keep people working by striving to get more business and by not replacing people lost through attrition. No one can guarantee that jobs will not be lost because of economic conditions, technological changes, or other factors beyond our control. However, all other things being equal, the improvements we make will make us more competitive and make our jobs safer. Therefore, we can make a policy commitment: no one will lose a job as a result of improvements we make in the system. If and when there is a layoff for any reason, the organization plans to lay off salaried and hourly people in direct proportion to their total number. If we do have to lay people off, we will give at least 60 days notice and do our best to place people with other organizations. In addition, people will receive a "Golden Handshake" which will at least meet the following minimum requirements..."

No one should make commitments they can not carry out. Sometimes only such a partial or complete commitment will get a stalled program going again. Its only drawback is that people are kept on longer than necessary until attrition absorbs the excess work force. But the continuing gains in most situations more than compensate for that expense.

USING THE FIVE HUMAN RELATIONS PROCESS CHECKS

Keep the above five questions in mind. Or even better, keep a list of them handy.   Ask these questions periodically and whenever you have to make a decision affecting people. If you come up with the "wrong" answer to any of the questions, reexamine the situation and see if there is a better way.

MORE WAYS TO KEEP PEOPLE MOVING AHEAD IN CONTINUOUS IMPROVEMENT 5, 10, or 20 YEARS AFTER STARTING THE EFFORT.

1) Have annual "Continuous Improvement" or "Quality" Month. During that month one or more members of senior management visit all areas of the organization, and does the following:
- hears reports on progress
- dispenses non-monetary awards, primarily to teams
- brings new ideas for improvement
- reviews plans for the following years

2) Have "natural work teams"—those people at all levels that work together—meet on a regular basis to review progress on eliminating troubles, problems, errors, waste and capitalizing on opportunities. Depending on level or area, these meetings may be daily, weekly, monthly or quarterly. Build consensus to do more.

3) Use most meetings (casual, business, official, unofficial) as a chance to ask about quality improvement and to help each other.

CHAPTER 9
TEAM UP WITH
CUSTOMERS AND SUPPLIERS

Both external and internal customers and suppliers are a part of your work process—a crucial part. You, your suppliers, and your customers have a common interest in producing a high quality, low cost product or service that customers want when and where they want it at prices they are willing to pay. The benefits are satisfaction for your customer(s) and more business and jobs for you and your suppliers. This customer-supplier relationship, both external and internal, is all part of the interfaces and interstices discussions on page 60. It is such an important subject, however, that we have set aside a special chapter to emphasize this relationship.

Look at the relationship as part of an overall system to accomplish an objective. Thinking of the overall system leads you to take your customers' and suppliers' needs into account in making decisions. By definition, the external customers determine what is value-added work. Therefore it is critical that you understand the customer's needs, both internal and external.

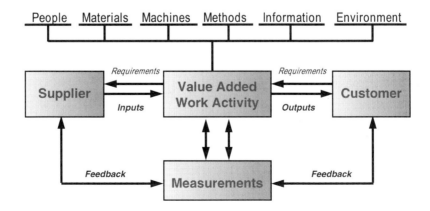

PRINCIPLES OF CUSTOMER AND SUPPLIER PARTNERSHIPS

Use the following principles to govern your customer and supplier partnerships:

- Communicate freely and frequently
- Use graphs and statistics to convert data to information as a part of the communication
- Understand the capabilities and needs of both suppliers and customers
- Let what your external customer wants from you guide you to value-added work
- Judge the needs of internal customers by whether those needs contribute to satisfying the external customers
- Avoid over-and under-specification by you or your customers
- Select suppliers who are already successfully practicing continuous improvement; if not available, select ones who will work with you closely. Select those that will work in real continuous improvement for consistent quality of products and services at low cost that meet your needs when and where you need them at prices you are willing to pay.
- Minimize the number of suppliers
- Substitute statistical evidence for incoming inspection whenever possible
- Select suppliers that have the ability to grow with your needs—capacity, technology, capital and geography.

Review this list and use it to check your process of working with suppliers and customers.

Different customer bases require different approaches. When you have a few large customers, it is relatively easy to maintain a dialogue with them. When you have a large number of customers (distributors or end users) called upon by your sales force, it is more difficult to find out what the customers are thinking. Reviewing and classifying complaints is important, but it doesn't go far enough. Conducting a telephone survey is a better way to learn about customers' needs and degree of satisfaction. Another useful device is the lost order report, which salespeople use to describe reasons they did not get orders. This report allows you to learn from a very important group—the people who should have become some of your customers, but didn't. In addition we need market research data on the customers with whom your sales/marketing people do not directly communicate.

If you sell a consumer product or service, you need a different approach to learn what the final customer is thinking. Large companies selling consumer products (and some politicians) use techniques such as focus groups or point of purchase questionnaires. Consumer service organizations, such as hotels and hospitals, present a different challenge. The written survey asking for comments is usually not effective, so people at such organizations must be innovative.

Case: A Free Breakfast

One hotel offered selected customers a free breakfast if they would have it with one of the hotel managers and discuss the facilities and service. The hotel tried to get seasoned travelers and found the breakfasts an excellent source of suggestions. Besides learning what the customers liked or didn't like about the hotel, the managers also learned about things that had impressed customers favorably or unfavorably at other hotels. They found out what pleased customers and compiled a good list of ways to make their hotel more attractive.

Continuous improvement can be an excellent sales tool. Look for suppliers who practice continuous improvement; some of your potential customers are looking for the same thing. A company was making a coated disc which was a critical part for manufacturers of computer memory disc drives. After they developed effective process controls, they began to show their customers how this could help them. In the next 18 months, their shipments increased by 78%.

CAVEAT EMPTOR IS OBSOLETE

Playing suppliers off against each other, viewing their claims with suspicion, trying to cut corners or withhold information to win a contract—all these tactics waste time, poison relationships, and eventually come back to haunt you. In continuous improvement, customers and suppliers work as a team. The objective of the team is the best possible process to deliver a product or service of high quality that meets the needs of the ultimate customer or consumer. When your suppliers and customers work smoothly with you, with mutual trust, the result should be a very effective team—a partnership.

More and more companies are undertaking vendor certification programs with their major suppliers. When the supplier meets the requirements for process control and continuous improvement, the customer treats the vendor's product as if it had been produced in-house. This allows further processing without incoming inspection. In the case of products for resale, the goods may be sent directly to distribution warehouses or drop shipped directly to customers. The savings in time and expense can be enormous. Other benefits come from better customer service.

As an example, a Quick Response (QR) system has been developed in the general merchandise industry that has produced dramatic results for merchandisers such as Wal Mart and their suppliers. This system was initiated originally by the "Crafted with Pride in the U.S.A. Council" as a competitive response to foreign suppliers. A supply chain analysis showed that lack of cooperation and information flow between suppliers and customers caused the supply cycle to be long, resulting in out-of-stock positions and merchandise markdowns. The overall loss to the system was projected at $25 billion! This study led to a strategy of cooperation between suppliers and customers which included electronically sharing point-of-sale information. It also included such techniques as generating automatic replenishment orders. This typically resulted in a 75% reduction in replenishment lead time. Pilot studies were done with Dillards, J.C. Penney and Wal Mart. All three pilots resulted in sales increases of 20-25% and improved inventory returns of 30% or better. Improving in-stock performance from 70-75% to 95+% created the sales increase; inventory improvement came from lower levels of safety stock. Customer satisfaction improved; increased sales allowed the reduction of prices. Each of the three companies in the pilot projects showed increased market share and increased profits. The grocery industry has started a similar program called Efficient Consumer Response or ECR. The ECR Working group estimates the potential savings at over 10% of sales! This comes from treating everyone in the supply chain as partners, and sharing information.

In 1980-1981, long before the current customer-supplier rage, we effectively utilized real supplier partnerships. Our supplier of a high-precision aluminum substrate for computer memory discs recorded the critical measurements of each part during manufacture. These data were fed into a computer which printed out a control chart of the process and a histogram of the product specifications in each shipment. These charts told us much more about the product than any incoming inspection could. We knew exactly what we were getting and could analyze how it would work in production. Working with the vendor, we asked that the range of one critical specification be lowered if possible. By concentrating on that parameter, while loosening the range on another, the vendor was able to make a significant improvement in the critical parameter, which improved our processing yield dramatically. These changes required close teamwork with the vendor. Just asking people to bid on specifications and inspecting to those specifications will not allow the close working relationship necessary for continuous improvement.

The enormous improvements in the quality and productivity of the work of many industries demonstrate the success of such partnerships with suppliers. The U.S. automobile industry has led the way in making improvements by changing supplier relationships, but businesses from chemical manufacturers to supermarkets have scored similar successes by working closely *with* their suppliers.

Many of the techniques of working with suppliers in a new way were developed in the auto industry. The old system of designing a car started with the styling and design group which specified the appearance and performance of the model. The engineering design groups developed detailed drawings and specifications for all the parts and sub-assemblies. Next, manufacturing and assembly developed their plans, developed the tooling and bought new equipment required. Finally, detailed specifications for parts were sent out to outside suppliers for bids. The purchasing department attempted to squeeze the lowest possible bid from as many as 2500 suppliers, including in-house parts departments. Design and engineering of the car and its parts were done in sequential steps with each group performing its function, setting design criteria and engineering specifications with little or no input from the people who have to manufacture the parts or assemble the cars.

Now most auto companies have moved toward a system of simultaneous or concurrent engineering. Suppliers and internal manufacturing groups are consulted during the design and engineering process so that the car is designed to optimize the cost by getting ideas from all the people involved and working together to engineer the highest quality, lowest cost functional solution to each design issue. Often suppliers are entrusted with the complete design and fabrication of a component such as seating, which is their area of expertise. This approach usually results in a better, lower-cost product and has the additional advantage of reducing the number of suppliers for seating parts from, perhaps, 25 to 1.

The supplier's engineers and the internal engineering team

work together on value engineering to ensure minimum costs. Typically, they also agree on objectives for cost reductions over the life of the model. Savings from these reductions are shared between customer and supplier. Savings beyond those objectives due to the supplier's diligence and creativity often accrue substantially to the supplier. Recognizing those ground rules encourages sharing of information between supplier and customer. Both work together on continuous improvement in meeting customer needs with high quality products at the lowest possible cost.

A further benefit of a close relationship comes when the customer develops sufficient confidence in the supplier to accept parts and assemblies without inspection. When a problem does arise, all work together to get to the source of the problem to assure it does not recur. Just-in-time deliveries reduce inventory requirements and force quick resolution of problems as soon as they arise.

In many industries, not working closely with suppliers is often the # 1 or # 2 cause of waste.

CHAPTER 10
IMPROVE CONTINUOUSLY...
FOREVER

In the old way of working, successful completion of a major project often means celebration, a period of rest, and then, often, a return to the status quo. But the quality revolution is not a one time study; it is a new way of thinking about problems and improvement that becomes a part of your daily thinking. You do it at every level of the organization—not just the low level work. People at lower levels seldom have the knowledge or power to institute or recommend these big changes. Yet we need people changing and improving at every level.

What do I mean when I talk about doing it all the time? It is continuously questioning why things can't be better, what you can change to make them better. It is eliminating the idea of maintaining the status quo, of defensiveness and criticism. It is about people comparing the way things are now to the way they could or should be. It will take time and a great deal of effort for people to change the way they think, work, talk and act. But the results are well worth the effort.

KEEP IMAGINEERING!

Use imagineering to release the power of the people. People's brains, time and energy are waiting to be tapped, and imagineering gives them the opportunity. They respond to imagineering by collecting data, having open discussions, and getting everything out on the table. The contrast between the old system and the new system is huge. Making imagineering a permanent part of everyone's work is not easy, because it takes a change in the way people think. But once you get beyond the initial resistance, and see what it can do, the snowball will roll. Over time, imagineering will become a hugely powerful tool for everyone to use all the time. Use it at all levels of the organization.

MORE SOPHISTICATED WORK

After working for three to five months, you should be:

- Refining some of the techniques and making them a part of your everyday activities and way of thinking
- Using the tools to establish a framework for continuous improvement
- Becoming more sophisticated in the use of tools.

This happens when managers are committed to the new system, when they provide the necessary training, and when they lead by example.

Throughout this process, focus on time. Become conscious of time as the raw material that you work with in all of your activities. What do you want to do with that raw material? You want to perform value-added work. And you want to continuously improve the effectiveness with which you perform that value-added work. Remember the chart on page 77 of the types of work. Typically, 25% or less of the time is spent on value-added work. And value-added work is the only real thing that counts. It includes everything that you really want to accomplish. So make these two concepts—time and value-added work—a part of your everyday thinking. Ingrain them in the way you think, talk, work and act. Time is your raw material, not to be wasted. And value-added work is your finished product.

Within a few months take the data you obtain from your work sampling studies and make detailed flow charts of your operations. Flow charting is useful for understanding what the processes of work are, for agreeing on them and communicating them, and for seeing how they can be changed and improved. Initially, management may be making the flow charts and interpreting them, but everyone should be trained to make them, so that they can use them to eliminate work which does not add value and improve the way they perform the value-added work. The charts done by each person do not need to be sophisticated or even 100% accurate. One of the major benefits in getting people to use flow charts is to get them to think about what they are doing and how they are doing it. They will discover many areas where they could do things differently and/or do different things to improve the process. Use flow charts on a regular basis to communicate ideas about the way work is being done and to solicit ideas for improvement from others. But senior managers must lead the effort to study and change the really big and key processes that only they can change.

KEEP THE WASTE OUT

Once you have made good progress in eliminating the waste in the work of your department, work station, business unit or entire organization, how do you keep it out? How do you prevent new inefficiencies and new unnecessary work from creeping in? By changing the way you and the people you work with think, talk, work and act. Think of time, think of value added by the work. Use work sampling and flow charts so you always understand what is happening. Use methods analysis and imagineering to make continuous improvements. Recognize that improvement is continuous, not just a one-time affair. Improving continuously may sound simple to do, but it isn't.

How do you help others to work in this new system of management? Why should they want to cooperate? Do they see a benefit in making the effort to change? Helping people requires leadership, a sensitivity to people's needs, and a fostering of pride in individuals and in the organization. Leadership is key. The leader is the one who is out front leading the charge. He or she shows by example and uses the tools and concepts to improve his or her work. At the same time, the leader is using his or her knowledge and the resources of the company to train other people to use the same tools and concepts.

If you understand the power of these tools, you will be able to impart your knowledge and enthusiasm to others. But the only way to understand the tools is to use them yourself. Then you are in a position to coach others. Play on the team. You may be calling the signals, but also participate in the plays. People will not be willing to help change the status quo merely because you ask them to, if you, as the leader, are not changing your own actions.

Be sensitive to people's needs. One of their primary needs is security. Another is the need to understand and participate in decisions that will affect them. Don't let this process be seen as a program for "chopping heads" or for making people work unusually hard. Make people aware of the plans for the organization as waste is eliminated. Show them how the plans will keep the company competitive and/or leading the pack. We may at times, because of big changes in the business or major process changes, have to reduce people. The keys to doing this fairly and in the best interests of people and the organization are as follows:

- Have people educated in Continuous Improvement and working in it well in advance
- Follow the "golden rule"
- Use your best efforts to sell more products and/or services
- Get out new products and services
- "Shut the front door" (no hiring)
- Use attrition
- Help people get new jobs internally or externally
- Maintain open communication as to what is going on in the business and why
- But when you have to do it, do it quickly

I have never met a person who would rather do useless work than useful work. People would rather spend their time doing value-added work than non value-added work. People want to feel they contribute. It is management's duty to provide full-time value-added work. When management does this effectively, then people will be able to take pride in what they accomplish each day.

People who take pride in their work will also be proud of the whole organization. They would much rather work for an industry leader than a company heading for or in bankruptcy! Growth and improvement are their own rewards. Improving the way you do things means more opportunities for growth. This in turn means new chances to improve the way you do things, and so on. When you meet someone who works for a very successful company, you expect them to be proud of it. On the other hand, if you meet someone who complains about their organization, you will guess that the organization is not doing well. Pride, continuous improvement, and success usually go hand in hand.

There are really two major phases to "improve continuously....forever." They are Phase 1—Build the infrastructure for constant improvement during the first 1-2 years. Change the paradigms. Educate the people. Get teams going on waste. Then comes Phase 2 in the following years—move toward World Class and sustain the leadership and effort. (See description on page 100.) Continue as a learning organization, finding and eliminating more waste in bigger clumps everywhere. Integrate the major process changes (major management innovation) into continuous improvement on a regular basis. Drive for bigger and much more customer and supplier partnerships for truly big cost reductions, time reductions, quality, and reliability improvements. Have every business unit and person understand and use the value added work concept including measurement.

CORE VALUES

Some organizations work with a set of core values. I suggest that we include in those core values continuous improvement and sharing. At the Ready Bake Division of Weston Foods in Canada, these two values are linked together—share the savings of continuous improvement with customers, shareholders and employees. This is a meaningful commitment to most people.

TWENTY-FIRST CENTURY QUALITY

If this book achieves its purpose, it will multiply the rate of progress your organization makes in achieving real Continuous Improvement. But knowing how to do it will mean nothing without leaders at all levels making a major commitment. A few years ago Jim Copley and I met Dr. Deming in an airport and we discussed why Western companies weren't making more progress in Continuous Improvement. Dr. Deming said, "It's three reasons: #1 is leadership, #2 is leadership and #3 is leadership!"

The process of making a major change is never easy. Without committed leaders very little will change, particularly the big things that include the vital few. I hope the people reading this book will make the commitment to help their organization change and adopt Continuous Improvement on all the work and work processes to please external customers and do it with low costs and high productivity.

How to do it is straight-forward, but it isn't easy. A sustained, aggressive effort will bring amazing results. Quality will rise, costs will go down, and customers will be delighted. Employees will be motivated and fulfilled.

The best plan for any organization in the next century—provide the best possible product or service at low cost that customers want at the most appropriate price. I have had the opportunity to sell major products and services that were based on this plan several times. What fun! Everyone works together for the common goal. Everyone is aligned. Naturally it leads to growth and opportunity for everyone. Relentless dedication to this plan will ensure success.

Toyota summed up the philosophy of this book succinctly. One of its advertising slogans is "**THE RELENTLESS PURSUIT OF PERFECTION!**" Today more and more Western organizations are doing the same thing! Join them now.

IS REAL IMPROVEMENT INCREASING? ARE WE IMPROVING THE PRODUCTIVITY OF OUR PEOPLE? THE QUALITY AND DELIVERY OF OUR PRODUCTS AND SERVICES?

In 1973-1974 at Nashua Corporation, we established a Profit Improvement Program (PIP) for the Corporation and all of its parts. We had learned about this program from Emerson Electric Company and the publicity that surrounded their very successful "Improvement Process." We were also getting sketchy information about improvement in Japan. Each operating division and corporate staff group had its own PIP. Within these groups each plant, department, engineering and R&D group, sales force, financial and/or administrative group, had its own PIP as part of a larger effort. The total of these efforts was the Corporate PIP. These efforts were closely monitored by top/senior management but run and measured by the operating and staff group managers. Top/senior managers were involved in some of the early projects. They all contributed to the overall PIP effort which had brief and simple (1 or 2 pages) monthly, quarterly and annual reports. The annual gains for the company were in the range of 2-4% of revenue ($300MM to $675MM revenue or gains of $6MM to $25MM/ year during the 1973-1979 period).

During this period we were buying $50MM to $150MM of product through Japanese companies who had been winners of the Deming Prize for Quality. From them we learned of tremendous improvement that came from strong, top management leadership and commitment for improvement, using a combination of statistical methods and industrial engineering. By early 1979 this led to inviting Dr. W. Edwards Deming to visit the senior management in Nashua, New Hampshire to discuss improvement. The main opposition to moving ahead with Dr. Deming's principles and theories was the success of our PIP programs. Our Chief Financial Officer stated that the PIP program was a terrific improvement process, far better than any he had seen in many years of field work as a senior person in one of the big accounting firms. Along with one or two other senior managers, I saw the tremendous potential of The Deming Method because it tapped much more heavily into all of the people - their brains, time, energy, and pride in achievement.

On March 9, 1979 we launched our "Quality Program" with Dr. Deming as our advisor. By the middle of 1980 we were being sought out by the top managers of the automotive manufacturers and their suppliers including the big chemical and electro-mechanical manufacturers of the USA.

They were regularly visiting us at Nashua Corporation on a weekly basis. It was appalling to learn how little work their organizations were doing in Improvement. Some were involved but primarily in areas of major capital investment and high technology. The study, change, and constant improvement of the work of people and machines and the associated work processes was minimal.

During this April 1979-April 1983 period of working the new way, the size, extent, and rate of improvement was far beyond our fondest hopes and wishes. Some operating divisions reduced their costs of goods sold by up to 15 percentage points (from 65% to 50%). In a flat market, one division increased revenue at a rate of 30% per year. Customer satisfaction in practically every division rose dramatically. These things happened because we lifted all the people up, helping them to be more capable, both individually and collectively, than we had ever dreamed. At the same time we made it in their interest to work the new way. Employee satisfaction was way up; absenteeism and turnover were way down. During visits with managers at other companies, we learned that most organizations badly needed to be seriously interested and active in Continuous Improvement.

Since "retiring" in April 1983 and forming Conway Quality, Inc., I have worked with and visited organizations all over the world for over 13 years. From 1983 to 1987 very few were working effectively in improvement. 1987 to 1991 was a period of great change, particularly in the USA. The education, training, and world competition of the 80's brought changes, improvements, and many good results. From 1991 to 1995 the changes and improved results have continued. In the USA today practically every organization is seriously into some form of improvement effort. It may be restructuring, reengineering, quality, productivity, leadership or continuous improvement. In most cases people have facts documenting some of these improvements. What these people and organizations need is further education, training, and help to improve both what they are working on and how they are doing the work. Most can still make quantum leaps in the rate and magnitude of real improvement.

Many good things have also happened in Europe, Latin America and other areas of the world. In my view, the rate of improvement in the USA is now the best in the world. While currency changes in value have helped the USA to be more competitive, the important and long-lasting changes are the changes in the work and work process led by top and senior managers and driven by people at all levels. We now are in a truly competitive world market. Japan, East Asia, USA and Canada, Latin America, and Europe all have their special strengths and weaknesses. Will the USA keep up and further improve its efforts in industry, commerce and government? What will be the world's competitive reaction to the USA lead in computers, telecommunications, biotech and aerospace as well as the rapid improvement effort? What does the future hold? Time will tell.

APPENDIX A
Step-by-Step Guide To
Work Analysis

In a typical situation, a manager or supervisor wanting to collect data, analyze, and change or improve the work in his or her area or unit would schedule the following steps and work with the people to complete them. We can break them down into two phases.

Phase I: Getting Started and Analysis:

1) Explain the process to all employees

2) Identify and write down all activities

3) Flow chart major activities

4) Classify activities into categories of work

5) Estimate times or collect hard data for activities and the tasks that make up those activities

6) Estimate the cost of each activity and task

7) Fix the obvious

Decide with the people involved. Can they finish the analysis and change alone? If so, let them do it. If not, form project teams or designate the work as part of a major reengineering effort. Steps 8 thru 11 are the basic steps included in the Conway Methodology for Eliminating Waste (*The Quality Secret*, page 126). These steps are also the basic steps covered in Reengineering-Major Management Innovations-chapter of this book. The entire cycle above, as well as the Conway Methodology and Reengineering Methodology is based on the Shewhart Cycle-Plan, Do, Study Act.

Phase II: Continuing Analysis and Implementing Changes

8) Question each activity and task
9) Imagineer
10) Prepare recommendations for improvement
11) Implement the improvements

The manager or supervisor should "schedule" these steps because it is important to have some time goals in mind and have measurements for progress. Otherwise the momentum is often lost. Depending on the complexity of the area involved, the above steps ordinarily take from three to nine months. While these steps tell how to get started, the effort does not end after the initial analysis. It should become a way of thinking about work processes and be done on a continuing basis.

We will discuss each of these areas, some in great detail. After reading this section, you should be ready to begin analyzing work.

Step 1: Explain the Process

All the people in the work unit or area need to understand just what is planned—the reasons for this process, how you plan to go about it, and what effects it may have on the area. This step is important because the cooperation of the people is necessary for a truly successful process. A good first step will convince people that it is in their interest to cooperate and that they will not be punished for helping to discover the waste that exists in their work, since it exists in everyone's work.

Emphasize that:

• The purpose of the effort is to make continuous improve-ment in the work processes to better serve customer (client) needs and to make the organization more effective in meeting those needs. The organization wants to grow by selling more at lower costs.

- The key to continuous improvement is to find, quantify and eliminate waste of material, capital, time and opportunities.
- Time is wasted in all organizations, and most of that waste is the fault of the systems in which people work.
- To find the waste, you need to make a detailed analysis of what is being done now.
- By eliminating the waste and rework, you improve the quality of the product or service that comes from the work. Thus you will have happier customers who will want to continue to do business with you and buy more.
- The purpose of the analysis is not to lay blame or to make people work harder. It is to help people work effectively on the right things, on the things that count. The organization will grant amnesty for any past mistakes.

Step 2: Identify Activities

After explaining the process, identify all the activities being performed, the major types of work being done in your department. Think about what your department does that produces a product or service for a customer. Although this customer is often an internal one, keep in mind that true value-added work provides value to the <u>external</u> customer. Obviously some support activities are necessary to provide products and services to external customers. But to eliminate unnecessary activities, test them to see if they provide value to the external customer.

First, help people to identify all their activities. Pass out the forms, if any, and ask them to spend 15 to 30 minutes trying to think of all their work activities and writing them down. Emphasize that you are not going to judge them by what they list. You are merely trying to identify the work being done. Everyone should expect to find waste; that's what you are trying to identify. You are not trying to punish anyone, but to get information to find the waste and eliminate it. No one likes to feel they are doing useless things. You are trying to arrange to do more of the things that add value and fewer or none of the things that don't add value.

Be available to answer questions. After each person has had a chance to prepare a preliminary list, go over it with him or her and suggest activities he or she may have forgotten.

Now **you** do the same. Take a piece of paper and make a list of your own activities. Remember, the objective is to cover everything you do during your working day except for personal time, scheduled breaks and lunches. Include lunch time activities if you have working lunches or sometimes entertain customers then. Remember our definition of activities—those functions that are performed to accomplish a purpose, usually to provide a product or a service. I distinguish that from tasks—the items of work you do to accomplish an activity. Emphasize that you especially want to identify any activities that they might consider to be wasteful, in whole or in part. Reiterate often that the purpose is not to be critical but to examine the work process to see where the system should be changed. When appropriate, remind them about weekly, monthly and annual activities and any types of one-time assignments they may receive.

An example of a list is shown. This list is for a customer service representative. Notice it is a simple listing of activities as they occur to a person thinking about what he or she does. All the activities are listed in terms of the purpose of the activity.

1. Take order from customer over phone.
2. Make computer credit check.
3. Enter order in computer terminal.
4. Answer customer pricing and delivery inquiries.
5. Answer customer complaints on late delivery, shipping errors, billing errors.
6. Attend meetings.
7. Be trained on new products.
8. Attend other training.
9. Call customers to remind them to order and to suggest new products.

10. Answer inquiries from sales force re: order status.
11. Fill out complaint reports.
12. Fill out claims reports.
13. Fill out late order report.
14. Fill out customer activity report.
15. Discuss work with supervisor.
16. Call customer to discuss change in delivery schedule.
17. Make weekly and monthly summary of claims status.
18. Inform sales force of claims meeting.
19. Attend weekly claims meeting.
20. Print out and file orders.

Note that the list says "Take customer order over phone," rather than "Talk on phone." And item 12 reads "fill out claims report," rather than "do paperwork." Sometimes you have to leave out the purpose, as in #6, "attend meetings," because you know there are going to be meetings but are not sure of their purpose. If you attend a regular meeting, as in #19, "Attend weekly claims meeting," list that separately.

Don't worry too much about whether the lists are filled out perfectly. The main purpose is to identify all the things people do. The rule is "If first in doubt, write it down." You can always edit them and put them in logical order later. Help people to feel free to put down everything, even those things they may think they shouldn't be doing, or that are a waste of time. In fact, you especially want those types of things, because they cause waste. Make sure that people understand that you expect to find waste and that amnesty is given for any past mistakes.

Here are a couple of examples. Taking an order from a customer over the phone is an activity. Making copies of that order or filing it are tasks within that activity. Filling out a customer order report is an activity. Looking up data in files is a task within that activity. For now, you are only interested in activities. We will come to tasks when we discuss flow charting of activities. Start with daily activities, but also include weekly, monthly, and annual activities and any types of one-time activities.

It's not easy to sit in a room away from your work and think of what you do all day. Actually it is a lot easier if you do it over a period of time in your own work environment, but even then it's hard to think of everything.

Examine your list to see if you listed an activity that you would classify as unnecessary. Did you list "attending meetings" as an activity? Would you consider all the time spent in meetings as value added? more than 50% of meeting time? more than 25%? Did you list a considerable number of items either preparing or reading reports? How much of that eventually benefits your outside customers, OEM's, distributors, dealers, retail stores and consumers? How much time is spent in communications? Look at your list and estimate how much of your time is spent in meetings, reading and preparing reports, reading mail, writing letters, discussing things with your employees, your boss, and your peers. How much of that time is value-added from the customer's viewpoint? How much of it is even necessary for the operation of your organization?

One of the biggest objections to undertaking continuous improvement is "I'm too busy already. I don't have time to work on continuous improvement." When you review your work in considerable detail, you will find that there are unnecessary, low-value and no-value tasks that you can work to eliminate, saving the time to concentrate on permanent improvement in the way you work. Seeing the savings that will be possible over time encourages people to do the initial extra work.

After all members of the group have completed a preliminary list, ask them to keep the list handy and add to it as they are reminded of additional activities by their actual work. Consider making your list public to encourage openness and demonstrate that everyone engages in non-productive activities. Help people with their lists. Encourage people to discuss them with others.

Next, consolidate and edit your lists. Group the lists from all the people with similar jobs. Compare them and then draw up one list for that particular group. Continue until you have an edited list for each type of job.

Combine these to obtain an overall department list. Some activities will involve several of the groups of people. For example, the activity "Prepare monthly cost variance report" might involve the standard cost clerks, the reports clerk and the assistant supervisor. The easiest way of thinking about activities is in terms of the products or services produced by each department. The number of activities may vary widely between departments, depending upon how diverse their responsibilities are. Ordinarily a department will have somewhere between five and fifty separate activities. Examples of activities are:

- resolve customer pricing complaint
- issue monthly budget report
- grant credit approvals
- prepare new product marketing analysis
- maintain standard costs for a product line
- pay weekly employees

Once you have a final list of department activities, you are ready for Step 3.

Step 3: Flow Chart Major Activities
Flow charting is a key tool in understanding and documenting any work process. A process flow chart is "The graphic presentation of the activities involved in the work process. These activities are shown in sequence by symbols with an accompanying description. Work and wait times are also shown." A good detailed guide to flow charting is found in Appendix E. *The Quality Secret* presents a summary guide on pages 88-95.

The key points in flow charting are: 1) it is sequential. That means you're taking the events in the order in which they occur, one step after another. 2) It uses a simple set of symbols to categorize all the different tasks within an activity or process. These symbols are shown on the next page. Flow charting the tasks shows how procedures, people, materials and machines work together to make something happen, to get an end result. And, 3) it includes the time the work takes, broken down into its elements. When important it will also include distance moved.

Process flow charts help visually identify the waste in the processes. While making a flow chart, don't put down the way you'd like it to be, or that you think it should be; put down what it actually is. Don't put down how long you'd like it to take, but how long it actually takes to do the tasks and what the total elapsed time is. You can, however, make an imagineered flow chart which shows how you would like the process to look.

A flow chart also visually highlights non-value added activities such as rework, inspection, delays, duplication, etc. When you see the specific symbol for waiting time, you know right away that that's not adding value for the customer.

The suppliers and customers for each process become clearer when the process is charted. Who are the suppliers? What do they provide? Who are the customers? If a process doesn't have a legitimate customer, or if that customer doesn't really need what is produced, then you don't need that process.

Flow charts serve as excellent communications tools. They help everyone to understand and provide a way to assure that everyone agrees about what is going on. You'll find it surprising; people think they understand how the process works now. People describe what they think someone is doing, or even how they themselves do something. Then they get the facts as to what is actually being done and see substantial differences. So the flow chart sets down the facts and helps to get agreement on them. It shows what the process is, what is being done, and how long it takes. Time is important, and the flow chart emphasizes time.

Symbols		Denotes	Examples
Diamond	◆	Decision	• is the part good? • is the supplier the right one?
Square	■	Control/ Inspection	• verify travel requisition • check time cards • inspect part • approve salary increase
Circle	●	Operation	• make a copy • type a memo • run a machine • interview applicant
Arrow	➡	Movement/ Transfer	• send data to mainframe • deliver material to next work station • transport goods to customer • walking/shipping
"D"	◗	Delay	• waiting time (for response, in line, for instructions) • down time
Triangle	▲	File	• file document, copy a floppy disk

Steps in Making a Flow Chart

There are ten steps to make a flow chart.

1. Decide what activity or function you are going to improve. Do this after talking to people, observing, and perhaps doing some simple work sampling. Then you have an idea as to where the waste is and you can pick an activity that you think you can improve.

2. Give the process a title. Choose this title carefully to describe and set the boundaries of the process you are going to study.

3. Learn in depth what is going on. To do this, talk to the people doing the work. They are the experts in the current process. Listen carefully to what they say and encourage them to bring up any problems that they have and areas of waste that they see. You might talk to the suppliers and the customers of this process to get all the background— to find out what troubles and problems they see.

4. Identify and document the suppliers and customers of each work process. Try to give the specific inputs and outputs related to both the customer and supplier. Suppliers may provide materials, people, equipment, or ideas. What are your requirements from your suppliers? How do those requirements match with what they actually provide? Who are your customers, and what are their requirements? How do your outputs match those requirements? How do you measure on a continuing basis to be sure inputs and outputs match requirements?

5. Write an initial description of each step in the process or activity. Make each description brief. Decide on what degree of detail you're going to use. Naturally it will be different for building a nuclear power plant than it is for watering the flowers. You may start off with a gross breakdown, if the process is a long, complex activity, and later break it down into sub-activities as needed.

6. Observe actual activities and times and record them on a process flow chart data sheet like the one on the following page. This data sheet shows the simple process of watering the flowers. Ask the people doing the work to perform this step, with the initial description worked out in step 5 as a guide. Make it clear that you want what is actually being done. You're looking for what people actually do when they're performing this activity and how long it actually takes them to do each step. This number can be in seconds, minutes, hours, or days, depending upon how finely detailed the tasks are. Ordinarily, for activities that

you repeat over and over and that occupy a great deal of your department's time, you want to get into pretty fine detail, and probably will want to measure time in seconds. Expect revisions in the preliminary list of tasks, because when people actually do the activity and record the time, they will see things that are different from what you first recorded. Also, different people will do the same job differently.

7. Use the flow chart symbols to map the steps in the process. Decide which of the six symbols listed on the form best represents each step and fill in that symbol on the chart.

8. Connect the symbols in a sequence to indicate the direction of the work flow. You're trying to make a map of the process so that everyone understands what is being done and the sequence of events. As you map your process you may have loops and branches. If you have an inspection at step 9, and the part or document passes inspection, you go on to step 10. If it does not pass, you "loop" back and repeat steps 6 through 9. Similarly, different decisions at an inspection or decision step lead to different branches for the rest of the process. For example, take the activity of watering the flowers. Perhaps you've found from experience that if there are a large number of bees on the flowers, they may take as long as an hour to leave. At that step you have a branch, and if you decide the number of bees is too great, you return to the house instead of watering the flowers.

9. Summarize the event times associated with each symbol or type of task and add up the total elapsed time. Take each type of task, such as transport, and review the flow chart, picking up all the tasks which are identified with an arrow (for transport or transfer). Add up the times. Do the same for decision, inspection, operation, delay, and file. Now you have the total time spent on each type of task. When you add all those totals you will have the grand

total elapsed time for the whole activity represented by the flow chart. For this purpose, ignore any loops. If you have one or more important branches, you may have a total for each separate major branch.

Process Flow Chart Data Collection   ☒ Present Method   ☐ Proposed Method

Subject Charted _Flower Watering_   Date _3/7/96_

_____   Chart by _JRH_

_____   Chart # _101_

Department _Town Water Department_   Sheet # _1_ of _1_

Time In Seconds	Chart Symbols	Process Description
45	○ ⇨ □ ◆ D ▽	Decide flowers require water
28	○ ➤ □ ◇ D ▽	Go for water spray container
48	● ⇨ □ ◇ D ▽	Fill container with water
30	○ ➤ □ ◇ D ▽	Walk to flowers with container
17	○ ⇨ ■ ◇ D ▽	Inspect flowers
20	○ ⇨ □ ◆ D ▽	Decide which flowers to water
23	○ ⇨ □ ◇ ▶ ▽	Wait for bees to leave
68	● ⇨ □ ◇ D ▽	Spray water on flowers
27	○ ⇨ ■ ◇ D ▽	Inspect flowers for disease
30	○ ➤ □ ◇ D ▽	Carry water spray container back to storage area
12	○ ⇨ □ ◇ D ▼	Store water spray container
22	○ ➤ □ ◇ D ▽	Return to house
	○ ⇨ □ ◇ D ▽	
	○ ⇨ □ ◇ D ▽	
	○ ⇨ □ ◇ D ▽	
	○ ⇨ □ ◇ D ▽	
	○ ⇨ □ ◇ D ▽	
	○ ⇨ □ ◇ D ▽	
	○ ⇨ □ ◇ D ▽	
	○ ⇨ □ ◇ D ▽	
	○ ⇨ □ ◇ D ▽	
	○ ⇨ □ ◇ D ▽	
	○ ⇨ □ ◇ D ▽	
	○ ⇨ □ ◇ D ▽	

10. Make a Pareto chart that shows the amount of time spent on each category. How much total time is spent on transport or movement, how much on delays, operations? The Pareto will show you.

The completed flow chart is an essential tool in analyzing the work. It helps you see where the waste is, it serves as a communication device in talking about the work, and once you imagineer, it helps you visualize the perfect process. For those who would like some practice in preparing a flow chart, Appendix E contains a case study which helps you to prepare a relatively simple flow chart.

Step 4: Classify Activities Into Five Categories

First list all the activities being done by a group.

Next, break each of the group's activities into the tasks and sub-tasks necessary to conduct those activities. Examples of tasks within activities would be type invoice, make copies, make a phone call, obtain approval etc. Break down these tasks finely enough so that you understand exactly what is being done. Step #3, making a flow chart, should have helped you to identify the tasks which make up the group's major activities.

Also list the tasks making up those relatively simple or minor unit activities which you did not flow chart. Finally, write down all other tasks done by the unit which do not fit clearly into any of the activities you have listed. If there are a large number of these "unassigned" tasks, you probably missed identifying one or more activities.

The process of identifying all the tasks is not easy. It requires time to think about the work, periods of keeping records of what is being done, and discussions with the people doing the work. You should end up with a description of all the work being done in the unit.

The next step is to classify all the activities and tasks based on their value or necessity. Use an analyzer form similar to the one shown. All the time spent by people in a work unit can be classified as value-added, necessary but not value-added, unnecessary (rework), unnecessary (other), and time not working either authorized or non-authorized.

Work/Time Analyzer©

	Categories of Work							
Specific Work Activity	**Value Added Work**	**Necessary Work** (Non-Value Added)	**Unnecessary Work** (Rework)	**Unnecessary Work** (All Other)	**Not Working** Authorized	Not Auth.	**Time of Observation**
Observations (Check Appropriate Work Activity)							
Total Obs.								

Position: _____ Name: _____ Date: _____

Value-added means that it adds value for the external customer. If the work is done for an internal customer, does it help that internal customer do something of value for the external customer? Is the work something the external customer would be willing to pay for?

There is a great deal of **necessary** work in any organization which adds no direct value for an external customer, but which must be done. For example, preparing payroll checks has no direct value to a customer but is necessary for the organization to keep running. I am not suggesting that you try to eliminate things like preparing payroll checks. However, since tasks like this do not add value to the customer, you don't want to do them unless you have to, and you want to minimize the time that these tasks take. One goal of this process is to set a framework for maximizing the time spent on value-added work and minimizing time spent on all other activities.

People usually underestimate substantially the time spent on **unnecessary work (rework)**, because it becomes ingrained in the way you do things and is accepted as part of the job. Everything that must be done because something was not done right the first time is rework: rekeying an invoice, repackaging an item, redoing a report. Even the example we used to discuss project work in Chapter 5, handling a customer pricing complaint, is rework. It is being done because the process allowed an error or because things were not explained properly to a customer.

Most people think they do not have any **unnecessary work (other)** in their organization. But ask, why is it necessary? For whom is it necessary? Who gets value out of it which ultimately helps the customer? You may discover that many tasks and some activities are no longer needed, if indeed they ever were needed.

The fifth category, **time not working**, will not be found on any list of activities or tasks. List the legitimate, "authorized," not-working times, such as vacations, holidays, breaks, and personal time. Also attempt to estimate the amount of other, "unauthorized," time spent not working. One of the most frequent causes of time not working is time spent waiting for work, often because of scheduling or work flow problems. Or perhaps the group has to be staffed to meet a peak load and consequently, for parts of a work cycle, people are waiting for work. In most cases a perfectly stable flow of work is not possible, but usually you can get a lot closer than you are to a steady work load.

Identifying the time wasted because of fluctuating work load provides an idea of the kind of opportunity you have to improve through stabilizing the work load—or by reassigning work or people among different work units. If you have a widely fluctuating work load and a stable work force, you are bound to have a lot of wasted time and/or a peak where people get tired. Recognizing the problem and looking for solutions can yield major improvements.

Now let's practice categorizing activities and tasks. On page 201 is a list of activities and tasks to categorize. In addition to the five categories of value-added, necessary, rework, unnecessary, and time not working (authorized and unauthorized), add a sixth—insufficient information. In this list, if you feel there is insufficient information to definitely categorize the activity or task, categorize it as "I.I.", but also mark what you think the most likely category is.

Think about these items. The goal of this process is to look at work in a different way—in terms of its value or necessity. Be skeptical. Does this task really need to be done? Does it add value? If not, can you get rid of it, or part of it?

After you have completed classifying the tasks, turn to pages 237, which shows how Conway Quality classified the same group. Several tasks have more than one answer since the classification may vary depending on the individual circumstances.

Approvals of expense reports are inspection operations and should be minimized. Sampling can often substitute for 100% inspection or 200% inspection. An audit may provide increased inspection, or it may be used on a sampling basis to eliminate the requirement for approvals. For instance, if the expense reports are almost always correct, sample them. If they contain many errors, train people, inspect and then sample.

Even some things that may appear to be absolutely necessary, such as "reimbursement of expenses," may be reduced or eliminated through the use of credit cards.

The first three sales call items are considered value added, since they ultimately help a customer understand the need for your product. The value added by the lunching and golfing is questionable, but if these activities provide the opportunity to make the customer comfortable with you as a supplier, then they can add value. Asking a customer to pay an overdue invoice may be necessary work or rework, depending on the reason for the late payment. Handling a quality complaint should obviously be classified as rework, as should explaining an invoice error.

In analyzing the accounting transactions, ask whether some—like the journal entry for monthly closing—could be done automatically. Are things like monthly accounting reports needed? How often? Activity-based costing helps to rid organizations of a lot of such unnecessary work.

Categorizing   time spent talking can be difficult.   It may be necessary to discuss with a supervisor things that affect your work, but it may not be necessary to discuss the same topics with other people.   Some social chatter is probably necessary to insure smooth communication and cooperation among employees. However, you should think about how much is needed. A large amount done other than during breaks and lunch may be a sign of scheduling problems, which cause people to be waiting for work. In some instances, people may be able to converse and work effectively at the same time.

Correcting errors is rework.   Trying to do something to prevent them is value-added work.

Among the payroll items, there are things which appear to be necessary, but which may not be, e.g. writing and distributing payroll checks may be eliminated by a direct deposit system. Cashing payroll checks may be a fringe benefit, but it is "time not working" for the company.

Making copies could be value-added, necessary, rework, unnecessary, or time not working, depending on the use of the copies.   Filing last year's sales reports may or may not be necessary, depending on who is doing it and for what purpose.

The purpose of this exercise is to make you think about the value and necessity of activities and tasks in an organized way.

Now go back to the list of your own activities that you made earlier and classify each activity. You may not have too many that fit into the unnecessary category, because the tendency, when you are away from your work, is to think of the most important things you do. As you go through the list, think of other activities or tasks within activities that are unnecessary from the customer's and the total company's point of view.

You may find it more difficult to classify your own work than to classify the list you just completed. The purpose of the last part of the exercise is to help you realize that working in this new way will save you time, although initially you will have to make extra efforts to analyze your work.

When coming up with a list of unnecessary tasks, you may discover one or more obvious things that can be fixed easily and immediately, just by deciding to stop doing something, to do something differently, or to change schedules. This is "fixing the obvious." As you analyze your activities in more detail, you may come up with some things that will make you think, "Now why am I doing that?" or "Why am I doing it that way?" If you haven't thought about the work being done in an organized and document-ed way before you'll probably identify some significant waste that can be eliminated very easily and quickly. Look at the work from the perspective of its value to the ultimate customer. In even the best of companies that study their work, there is significant unnecessary work and rework going on.

Step 5: Estimate Times for Activities and Tasks

The next step in the process is to estimate the amount of time spent on each activity. Do this in two ways. At the start use the simplified method of asking people to keep a running work record of how they spend their time. This method has limitations, because people forget to write things down or guess at how much time they spent doing a particular activity. However, it gets you off to a fast start and helps you identify the activities and tasks that are being done. After the initial estimate, use a more sophisticated system of work sampling to get more accurate information. On the next page is a simplified form which sets off the minutes of the day and allows each person to record (in a brief way) what he or she is doing, with tasks separated by a line showing the time of switching from one task or activity to the next.

Running Work Record

8:00		11:00		2:00	
8:05		11:05		2:05	
8:10		11:10		2:10	
8:15		11:15		2:15	
8:20		etc.		etc.	
8:25					
8:30					
8:35					
8:40					
8:45					
8:50					
8:55					
9:00					
9:05					
9:10					
9:15					
9:20					
etc.					

If the work being analyzed is very repetitive and uses a substantial percent of total time worked in a department, you may want to get the help of an industrial engineer to collect additional data for greater accuracy.

While performing step two (identify and write down all activities) and step three (flow chart all activities) keep running work records. This saves time and helps you identify all the things being done. The length of time to keep the work records will vary with the work unit and with the person within that unit. If the work is repetitive and the same every day, then perhaps two or three days of recording will be sufficient to get a good idea of what is being done. If work is more complex and includes weekly or monthly tasks, then two weeks or perhaps a month will be needed. You will have to estimate the time required for annual activities, such as budgeting.

Summarize data from the running work record. On the summary sheet enter the list of activities (not tasks) applicable to a particular individual. Ask that person to take his or her work records and put each interval of time under one of the classifications as in the example below.

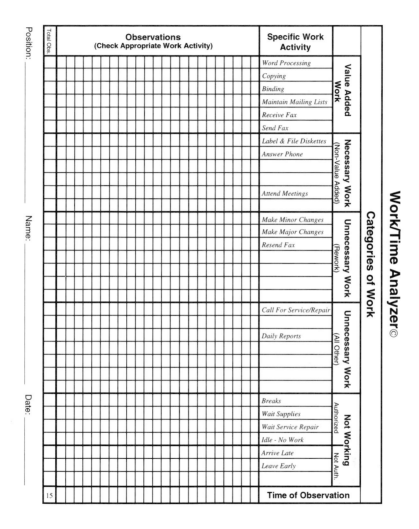

Next add all intervals of the time spent on a particular activity to get the total time spent on each activity. Then summarize and compute these as a percentage of total time spent. In other words, if the time record ran for three eight-hour days, or a total of 1440

minutes, and a particular activity, retyping incorrect invoices, took 60 minutes, then 60/1440, or 4% of the time was spent on retyping incorrect invoices. You need a fairly fine breakdown of activities to understand the work that is going on. But if any one activity totals much less than 3% of the total time of a person, the breakdown is probably too fine. Combine that activity with some similar activity.

A typical company making a study will come out with something like the pie chart below.

The Way We Work

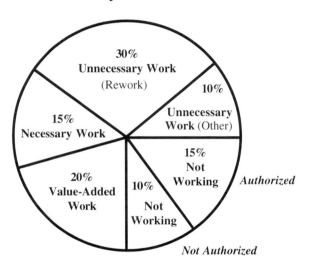

You may get something different from this, because a running record generally does not identify the waste as accurately as does work sampling. To get a reasonably accurate estimate of the time spent, you will need a work sampling study. Also, you have not yet factored in vacations, holidays and absenteeism. However, most people are shocked at the small amount of time spent on value-added work. It is nothing to be ashamed of. It is happening everywhere. But you cannot change it until you know how you are spending your time. To get a reasonably accurate estimate of time spent, you will need to do work sampling. See Appendix D.

Step 6: Estimate the Cost of Activities

The usual accounting system of accumulating costs of products or services does not help you find most of the waste. Each product or service is prepared by a series of activities. To find all the waste, examine these activities and compare their cost with the value to the organization and its customers.

Now estimate the cost of performing each activity and task. The actual approach varies depending upon what type of information you have available by department. The cost exercise is important for three reasons. First, nothing focuses people better than seeing the cost of something. Some people do their everyday jobs and direct others in their activities without thinking about the costs to the organization. Cost provides a common denominator to work with and identifies those activities that consume the most money. It helps set priorities.

Second, it helps to evaluate the benefit of each activity versus the cost. You may have second thoughts about how necessary or helpful some activity is, when you compare the benefits to the cost of that activity.

Third, this exercise will help to identify and quantify the cost of time spent not working. This time includes vacations, holidays, scheduled breaks and legitimate personal time on the one hand, and time not working due to peaks and valleys in work load, scheduling problems, poor work flow, and activities you have forgotten, on the other. This second category represents an opportunity for improvement. You have amnesty and you give amnesty to others. You are interested in improvement.

How do you estimate the cost of all your activities? First you need a list of all the jobs in the unit being studied. This is not a list of people by name, but a list of jobs by function. For example, take a typical cost accounting department and list the jobs.

Cost Department—Personnel Costs

Position	Hourly Cost
Supervisor	$20.35
Assistant Supervisor	$20.35
Std. Cost Analyst (3)	$13.20
Job Cost Analyst (4)	$13.20
Reports Clerk	$13.20

Next establish some broad salary or wage ranges for the jobs in question. These ranges are a rough guide, and don't be too concerned if you're not sure exactly which range fits a particular job. You're only looking for a rough estimate of costs— plus or minus 20%. Try to put all the people in the unit into no more than three different ranges. In the case of this cost department, we put them in two ranges—the Supervisor and his assistant in one range, and everyone else in a second range. The figures for average cost per hour in each range include the cost of fringe benefits, except for time off—vacations, holidays, etc. These costs will be shown separately as one category under "time not working."

Accumulate from your budget all the non-personnel expenses—telephone, travel, supplies, etc. Some of these you will be able to allocate to specific activities. For example, travel is usually identified with a particular activity, such as "making sales calls." Enter these in the first column under Non-personnel expenses, which is entitled "Specific Expenses." After you have allocated all the expenses you can to particular activities, you will have a remainder of budgeted expenses, such as office supplies, which are difficult to identify with one particular activity. Take the amount that is left and divide it by the total number of payroll hours to get a per-hour rate for these unassigned expenses. Then for each activity, and for time not working, multiply the number of hours by this rate, and enter the result in the second column under Non-personnel expenses, entitled "All Other." In this way you spread the rest of the expenses over the various activities. In the example shown you see a total of $63,000 of non-personnel expenses. $28,000 of that is allocated to specific activities, leaving $35,000 unassigned. Dividing that $35,000 by the 20,800 payroll hours yields a rate of $1.68 per hour for other, non-personnel expenses.

Cost Department--Non-Personnel Costs

	Specific	All Other
Travel		
Monthly Reports	$17,000	
Training	3,000	
Computer Time		
Monthly Reports	8,000	
Other		$12,000
Equipment		23,000
Total	$28,000	$35,000

Grand Total   **$63,000**

Other = $35,000/20,800 hours = $1.68/hour

How detailed should you be in your cost estimates? Should you estimate costs for groups of activities only, all activities, or all activities and tasks? The first approach, groups of activities, is probably not detailed enough, and the last, all activities and tasks, is probably too detailed. A good start is to cost all the activities, and then look at those major tasks within activities that you think might be modified or eliminated without a major effect on the activity itself. For example, take an activity such as "Prepare sales forecast." A task within that activity might be "Obtain from each salesperson an estimate of potential sales for each customer." If this is a costly task, you might want to weigh the benefits derived from it compared to the cost of obtaining it. In this case, cost the task separately as a sub category under "Prepare sales forecast." In any case, use your judgment as to how fine a breakdown you need. You want what is useful. Your goal is to evaluate the cost of your activities and tasks and compare that to their value to the company and its customers.

As you total the costs, you will begin to get a feeling of where your priorities should lie. The largest cost items should obviously be examined, but they will not necessarily give you the most opportunity for improvement. Use your judgment to set priorities; look at the costs, the categories of work (value-added and so forth) that each item fits, and your knowledge of what is possible. More will be possible than you first think. In the next stages of questioning and imagineering (which involve the most brainwork), the opportunities for improvement will begin to be identified. Many people will say "Why didn't I think of this before?" and "Why have we been wasting this time all these years?" Remember amnesty! Don't blame yourself or others, look on it as an opportunity for continuous improvement.

Often the biggest shock is when you add up the time spent on all the activities you have identified. When you add to that the time you spend not working because of vacations, holidays and so forth, and subtract the sum from the total payroll hours, you might be amazed at the time spent not working, or working on unidentified activities. If your organization is typical, you will probably have 10-15% not working because of fringe benefits such as holidays and vacations, and another 20% not working for all other reasons, most of which will be because people don't have full-time value-added or necessary work available at all times. There may be peaks and valleys that need to be smoothed out and there may be unnecessary overstaffing to meet peaks. You may have work flow problems, or scheduling problems. A major responsibility of management that has been almost unrecognized in industry is to smooth and schedule the work so everyone has value-added or necessary work available for them to do at all times.

Look at your list of activities and tasks, and your costs for activities, and perhaps some major tasks within those activities. Meet with one or two people and set up a preliminary list of priorities for study. When you have that list, you will be ready for the next phase, which is questioning each activity and task and then using imagineering to find ways to improve your work process.

Step 7: Fix the Obvious applies to work sampling, just as it does to flow charting. We mean those things that obviously need fixing, and for which an obvious fix is available. You are looking for the things that you can do quickly, to make a quick savings, without any great effort. If you find something that causes waste, can easily be changed, and is within your power to change, why not do it NOW?! Or if it is easy to fix, but you need someone else's approval or cooperation to fix it, don't wait! Go get the approval, and DO IT!! If it turns out that the problem is more complex and the solution less obvious than you had imagined, you can always postpone your solution and use the information you have gathered to work towards an eventual solution. Occasionally an obvious solution may turn out to be temporary or partial. In that case you will have to dig deeper into the process for further changes.

Keep a record of what you have done and what the benefits have been, in time saved, reduced errors, or whatever, so that it can be part of your report to management, "Things already fixed." Make this an action-oriented program. If something is obviously wrong, don't study it to death. Move ahead with implementation, where appropriate, throughout this process, and not just after weeks of data gathering and analysis.

However, for most cases you need to go deeper into the data. In Appendix D, on work sampling, we examine the causes of rework. In this case the single biggest class of rework is handling complaints—nearly half of the rework problem. How do you get at it? In this case you need more data. Find out what types of complaints cause the problem so that you can go after the causes and fix them. Go back and gather data either through more work sampling, by using other records you have available, or simply by asking people to keep track of the time spent on each type of complaint. In this case, the manager gathered the data and made another Pareto chart, shown on the next page, of time spent on complaints.

Customer Service Representatives - Complaints

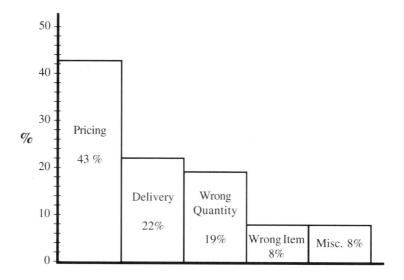

She found that pricing complaints took 43% of the total time used for handling complaints. She further calculated that handling pricing complaints occupied 7% of the entire workday for all of the people. It's easy to see that the company could save money by improving the systems and procedures for pricing and making sure that everyone understands the pricing, including customers, sales people, and customer service representatives. In this case, changes would save time in this department, and in other departments, and improve customer relations. Very often, eliminating rework improves the overall quality of the product or service and saves wasted time and material.

If this were a stand-alone work sampling study, you would go through two more steps. One would be to determine the sources of waste within the department and externally. The other would be to set up a project team to make improvements. Project work was discussed starting on page 103.

Step 8: Question Each Activity and Task

Review the list of your activities. Think about how the following questions might apply. All questions will not apply to every activity.

"What is its worth to the customer?" This customer may be internal or external, and in fact you may do most of your work for internal customers, but the ultimate measure of the activity's worth is its value to the external customer. The best person to judge the activity's worth is your external customer, so periodically ask him or her (and/or the people in your organization who deal with that customer) how useful or necessary this service is. It may be "nice" to have a particular service, but when you look at the cost of that service versus what it ultimately accomplishes for your external customer, you may decide it's not worth the cost in its present form. Then see if you can eliminate it or modify it in some way to reduce the cost and/or make it more useful.

"Is the purpose of this task still valid?" Is it really necessary, or does it really add value? There's the case of the janitor who mindlessly filled the President's water jug with ice water every day, even though no one ever drank anything from it. There are lots of similar things we all do that no one needs and which waste more time and money than that one. Apply this question to your own activities and to some of the tasks within those activities. Are they all still necessary? Were they ever necessary?

"What risks would you take if you eliminated it?" This is really a follow-up to the previous question. Often there is some risk involved in eliminating tasks or activities. The risk may be a nebulous one such as "everyone will not be fully informed," a risk associated with eliminating a certain report. Or it may be very specific, such as "credit losses may increase by up to 1%." This could be a risk associated with eliminating credit approvals for orders under $500. You then have to compare the risk and the savings to judge whether the risk is worth it. In some cases you cannot know until you try it, but there may be a small risk in trying it. If, for instance, you eliminate credit approvals for orders under $500, you can easily re-institute the approvals if you find your additional losses are greater than the savings. If you can easily change your mind if you find it doesn't work, try eliminating or simplifying activities. Can you eliminate all or part of your activities without undue risk?

"Can you transfer it to someone outside the company?" Obviously at less cost. This is often the case when someone outside the company is preparing paperwork that you have to duplicate. As an example, customers who are properly equipped may be able to enter purchase orders directly into your computer and generate savings for both of you. Or perhaps outside specialists can do specific tasks more cost effectively than you can. Some companies use outside specialist firms to audit freight bills. Are there any parts of your activities that might better be done by an outside firm?

"Can you consolidate the activity or task with some other job within the company?" We used an example earlier of combining a check of credit limits with the activity of entering an order. Can you combine some of your activities or tasks with others in your own department or outside the department?

Combine the next three questions, since they are related. **"Can you decrease the frequency of the service?"**; **"Can you reduce the content of the service?"**; and **"Can you reduce the number of people receiving this service?"** These questions can be applied to every service you provide. They are powerful because, the answer in almost every case will be "Yes." You *can* drop the frequency of the service. You *can* reduce the content of the service. You *can* reduce the number of people receiving this service. Such reductions may cause disruptions or bruised egos, but if you look at the value of what you are doing versus the cost in terms of frequency, content, or number of recipients, you can almost always streamline an operation.

These questions are most powerful when applied to two of the biggest time-wasters—reports and meetings. Decisions on reports and meetings—their frequency, content and recipients or attenders—are most often made on the basis of whether it would be "nice" for someone to know. Of course information is important, but only if it might be used to take action or make a decision. So when you question reports and meetings—their frequency, content and recipients or attendees—ask yourself if all the information they provide is needed, as frequently as it is provided, and by all the people who receive it. Will the information be used to take action or make a decision?

Reports are a major source of waste in most organizations. Each report or meeting by itself may waste only a minor amount of time, but when you add them all up, they are probably the biggest waste of time in industry and commerce. One of the world's fastest growing companies, Cabletron, holds meetings at waist-high tables, with no chairs.

Be ruthless in reviewing your reports and meetings. There is little risk in simplifying them. If you find you have gone too far, you can always re-institute a report or meeting. The waste in reports derives not only from preparing unnecessary information, but also from having people read unnecessary information. Think about reports that your unit prepares or receives, and make some notes as to which ones have the most waste. Then do the same for meetings.

Did you think of a report you could do without? How about reducing the content, to make it easier to prepare and/or easier to read? How about reducing the number of people or groups receiving the reports? Apply those three powerful questions to all your activities.

"Can you change the job so that a less skilled person can do it?" Once people begin doing a task on a regular basis, they think they must continue to do it forever. Review who is doing what and see if the skills needed to do a job can be downgraded—either by a simple reassignment, or by simplifying the job in some way to require less skill or knowledge. Over the long run the total cost of your activities will be less if you have more of them done by the appropriate skill levels. Also, job satisfaction will be greater when activities are properly matched with the skill and knowledge level of the person performing those activities. Can you think of any activities that you do, that someone at a lower level could do? Would that free up some of your time to do a better job of leading?

"Can you change the methods to make the job more efficient?" In the initial stages you are looking for obvious methods changes. Later on take a closer look with methods analysis, and perhaps enlist the aid of systems people and industrial engineers. For now, ask the simple question, "Are any obvious improvements possible by changing the methods we are now using?"

You will now probably think of other questions. Shortly we will talk about imagineering, which will help you develop more questions. But in this series, the last question is, **"Can you mechanize it or computerize it?"** This is the final question because you want to make as many improvements as you can before automating something. If you automate useless work, you will just accomplish nothing with less effort. While that may help reduce costs, it's not really what you want when you are trying to eliminate all waste. Automation can be very important, particularly with the low cost of computer power.

Now, here are the questions we just asked:

- What is its worth to the customer?
- Is the purpose of this task still valid?
- What risks would you take if you eliminated it?
- Can you transfer it to someone outside the company?
- Can you consolidate the activity or task with some other job within the company?
- Can you reduce the frequency of the service?
- Can you reduce the content of the service?

- Can you reduce the number of people receiving this service?
- Can you change the job so that a less skilled person can do it?
- Can you change the methods to make the job more efficient?
- Can you mechanize it or computerize it?

Step 9: Imagineer

After questioning the activities, use imagineering to further identify waste. You need to have lots of facts to be grounded in reality. It doesn't do any good to come up with pie-in-the-sky schemes that have no basis in the real world. Fortunately the process we have been discussing includes a great deal of fact gathering, which will provide you with the ingredients for successful imagineering.

First, take a detailed look at what you are doing now. Next, use tools such as Pareto charts and histograms to help you put the facts into a form that everyone can see, understand and use. This will give you an ideal takeoff point for imagining what everything would be like if it were perfect. As you look at each activity and task you are performing, ask, "Would we need to do that if everything were perfect?" or "How would we do this differently if everything worked perfectly?" If all of the people in the unit have just spent some time thinking about what work they are doing and classifying and documenting it, they are sure to have ideas for improvement.

So first you need facts. Help everyone to understand that the objective is not to criticize the past or the present but to understand the present so that you can make improvements in the future. Hold discussions in an atmosphere where all ideas are wanted and needed. A commitment to this process includes bringing out all problems without attaching blame to them. So you should bring up problems without fear of being criticized, but you should also bring them up in a non-critical way. Don't be saying "Aha! Here's my chance to point out what a lousy job this department has been doing."

Besides lots of facts and an open atmosphere, you need everyone in the act! Management or other people can't do this job alone. You need the ideas and contributions of all the people in the organization. Why? Because, as Dr. Deming said, they are the "experts." They know where the troubles and problems are, because they are the ones that encounter them on a daily basis. Without the support of those "experts," you will make much less progress. Besides their ideas, you also want their cooperation. They are the ones who will make the new or improved way work or fail. The best way to get everyone's support is to make them part of the process.

Step 10: Prepare Recommendations for Improvement

If you have gone through the first nine steps in the work analysis in enough detail, what to do and how to do it usually become obvious. If they are not obvious, you may need more data or more imagineering.

Most major changes require approval of someone else in the organization. In any case, before you implement a change, it is a good idea to write down exactly what you plan to do, what resources you will need, and what schedule you plan to follow. This document can then serve as your request for approval as well as your implementation plan. Pay particular attention to the resources you require. If continuous improvement projects are underway throughout the organization, there may not be enough people or money to support all of them at once. People coordinating the continuous improvement effort need to know the resources required so that they can set priorities.

Step 11: Implement

When you have the authority and the resources to undertake a particular action, set priorities and get to work. Don't wait until a study is completed before acting. As things that need to be done become obvious, set priorities and implement.

If an action requires approval, have your plan well prepared so that you can answer any questions, make any needed modifications, and move into action quickly when you receive approval.

VA	Value Added
N	Necessary
RW	Rework
UN	Unnecessary
NW	Not Working
II	Insufficient Info

Categories Of Activities & Tasks

_____   Fill out expense report
_____   Approve expense report of subordinate
_____   Provide second approval of expense report
_____   Audit approved expense report
_____   Pay reimbursement of expenses
_____   Prepare for sales call on potential customer
_____   Make sales call on potential customer
_____   Make phone calls to get appointments with potential customers
_____   Travel to present customer's office
_____   Take customer to lunch
_____   Play golf with customer
_____   Present new product information to customer
_____   Take order from customer
_____   Ask customer to pay overdue invoice
_____   Resolve customer quality complaint
_____   Explain billing error to customer
_____   Explain forthcoming price increase to customer
_____   Prepare journal entry for monthly closing
_____   Compute standard cost variances
_____   Prepare monthly profit and loss statement
_____   Print and distribute monthly accounting reports
_____   Prepare annual budget
_____   Correct mistaken accounting entry
_____   Take physical inventory
_____   Prepare sales tax return
_____   File amended tax return
_____   Talk to supervisor about your health problem and absenteeism
_____   Talk to supervisor about your new baby
_____   Talk to fellow employee about your new baby
_____   Talk to fellow employee about your health problem
_____   Talk to supervisor about ball game

_____ Take a sick day because you deserve it
_____ Discuss errors with another department with supervisor
_____ Correct errors made by another department
_____ Prepare a report on last month's shipping errors
_____ Prepare a report on last year's shipping errors
_____ Prepare a report on today's shipping errors
_____ Keep a run chart on level of unresolved customer complaints
_____ Make a Pareto chart of reasons for claims
_____ Prepare a weekly payroll
_____ Write weekly payroll checks
_____ Distribute weekly payroll checks
_____ Cash weekly payroll checks
_____ Prepare a report which no one uses to make a decision or take action
_____ Prepare a report of sales by product line
_____ Make copies on copy machine
_____ Wait in line at copy machine
_____ File last years sales reports
_____ File last years tax return

APPENDIX B
Developing The Continuous
Improvement Attitude

Continuous change for Continuous Improvement and involvement of all the people to promote that change requires a major shift in attitude for most organizations. The attitudes of managers and how they communicate those attitudes to others are key to making a change. More than a fifteen years ago, the *Economist* magazine, in the February 23, 1980 issue, described the difference between the new and old attitudes:

"The main secret behind any economic or social advance is the simple one of a relentless daily productivity hunt. The dividing line between successful and disastrous organizations in the world today is between those where the working force plans hourly for greater output tomorrow (call these enterprising) and those where most people are concerned to avoid any bothersome disturbance tomorrow (call these bureaucratic)."

Unfortunately, many organizations still lean toward bureaucracy, striving to avoid change rather than seeking continuous change. Even organizations that say they welcome change often shy away from it when it becomes uncomfortable. And some organizations lose the chance to benefit from much of the potential change when they assume that ideas for improvement and change should primarily come from those controlling the major systems and processes, the managers, rather than from the people working in the system who see in detail what is happening in each process. These people who are closer to the work also control many minor or smaller processes, where they decide what to work on and how they do the work.

The new attitude requires enlisting everyone in the search for change, for ways to eliminate waste and therefore continuously improve quality and customer satisfaction and lower cost.

THE KEYS TO MOTIVATION

Desire and commitment are vital to any major change. The greater the change, the greater the commitment required. Organizations make that commitment for many reasons, the most urgent and prevalent of which is the need to attain a leadership position in an increasingly competitive world. Many organizations are dissatisfied with their present management system and have found that minor or marginal changes are not effective in solving their problems. Others want to change because they aspire to be the best.

First Key—Dissatisfaction with the Present

Whether from desperation or aspiration, dissatisfaction with the present is the first key to change. Organizations must identify the difference (the Delta) between current conditions (current reality) and the conditions that could or should be if everything were right. From this difference usually comes the will to make a major change.

Second Key—Availability of a Better System

The second key is to discover and learn about the real continuous improvement system of management so that you believe in it enough to make a major commitment. This is the most difficult step of all. How do you abandon ingrained patterns of action for a new, unfamiliar system? You can only do that if you become convinced that the system works by studying it and learning why it works so well and trying it yourself.

Organizations of all types throughout the world have accepted the system I described in my book, *The Quality Secret,* and proven that it works effectively. This system is based on the principles taught by Dr. W. Edwards Deming. The Japanese, led by Toyota, first proved on a world industry scale that it works, and works incredibly well. Furthermore, many Western companies and subsidiaries of Japanese companies have proven that the system is transferable to Western culture. It has been successful in high tech and low tech, large organizations and small, government and non-profit, service, manufacturing and distribution. The system is not experimental. It has been proven for over 50 years.

Third Key—Know How
The third key to change is to know how to go about making the changes. The purpose of this book is to supply you with that knowledge.

The Mind Set for Change
The first change required is to adopt three important attitudes:

- Belief in continuous improvement
- Respect for people
- Intolerance for waste

Ingrain the search for **continuous improvement** in your thinking. This is the most crucial attitude change required. Almost everyone favors improvement—so long as it doesn't cause any disturbance in the way they have always worked. Consequently, improvements tend to come slowly and gradually, if at all.

Continuous Improvement, on the other hand, requires continual change, which can be uncomfortable, but you can replace the desire for a comfortable way of working with the joy of achievement. Just as a member of a sports team gets a thrill from a good play, a person doing a job can get a thrill from contributing to an improvement. The successful team member works continuously to improve the team's performance.

Groups or individuals can achieve much greater job satisfaction through continual improvement than by doing the job in the same old way. But it is not easy to make that transition. People have to see that it works and experience the joy of achievement before they become truly dedicated and try every day to improve the processes by which they do their work. The most successful companies, whether Toyota in automobiles or Federal Express in overnight shipping, have an almost religious devotion to continuous improvement. They may do it in different ways, but they are always seriously trying to improve through Continuous Improvement.

Respect for people is a crucial part of the continuous improvement system, not a negotiable benefit, as it often seems to be in organizations working the old way.

Intolerance of waste is a key part of the new attitude, and it results from understanding how much waste current processes produce and how that waste undermines the organization's goals. Two sections of Chapter 2—"The Core Activity" and "Finding the Waste"—focus on developing this intolerance to waste.

Obstacles to Overcome

There are two major obstacles to spreading these attitudes. The first is resistance to change. The second is the natural question, "Will this be good for me personally?" In almost all cases, the answer to that question is "Yes." First, continuous improvement brings joy in achievement, increased self-respect, and job satisfaction. Second, the only real employment security is the ability to produce quality products and/or services that customers want at prices they are willing to pay and at low cost. This is becoming increasingly apparent in today's competitive global environment. However, it is not always easy to convince people to change, or that change will be good for them. This requires both education and leadership. At the same time, people need a forum in which to raise concerns and questions.

Managers and executives need help to change first, or others will not follow. It is best for them to convince themselves, through study, trials, and talking to others, that the system of management for continuous improvement works.

How difficult it will be to spread the word greatly depends upon the past history and culture of the organization, including:

- The way people have been treated in the past
- Employment security practices
- Amount of waste built up in the organization

- Weight of the bureaucracy
- Past use of constructive studies and actions to improve work and work processes
- Leadership practices
- Promotion, pay and performance review system
- Management style, i.e. "help, coach and lead" vs. "tell, judge, control"
- History of past improvement efforts
- Amount of mutual trust among people at various levels of the organization
- History of working with external suppliers

All of these factors may need some change before the organization can completely adapt to the new system. Mutual trust is key in determining how quickly change will occur. If some practices have caused people not to trust management, those factors may need changing before people will cooperate in adopting continuous improvement. If management does not trust the people, managers will not be able to obtain and use effectively the ideas from people at every level. Every organization is different. Assess which of these factors need to be changed to gain trust and acceptance for the new system of management in your organization.

The Right Attitude

The path to success for an organization is to produce, consistently and at low cost, quality products and/or services that external customers want at prices they are willing to pay. Continuous improvement in all the work and work processes is the key to improving quality and reducing cost simultaneously. The key to continuous improvement is intolerance for waste—identifying, quantifying and eliminating waste in all forms through continuous process improvement as the core activity of the organization. To find and eliminate the waste you need the active participation of all the people doing the work, since those closest to the work can see the waste, troubles, problems, and complexities, and can suggest ideas for improvement. Leaders lead by personal example and by coaching.

APPENDIX C
Education And Training
For The Revolution

No one is likely to achieve substantial results working the new way without having completed a major program of education and training. There are several paths that a person may take from initial interest to the necessary level of commitment. These paths usually come from some combination of education and observation of what other organizations have done.

In the following discussion of education and training programs, I assume that one or more people who are in a position to make things happen are committed. Once this has happened, establish a group to organize and oversee the education and training of the rest of the organization. This group, often called a steering committee, usually includes at least one person with authority to commit the organization's resources. Ideally it also will include someone with a background in education, training and human resources.

The committee can make use of a number of resources. It can send people to seminars or, depending on the size of the organization, hold one or more private seminars. Seminars are particularly beneficial for people at the second level of management and above.

Front-line workers and their supervisors should attend an abbreviated seminar totaling six to eight hours. These seminars can be conducted by outside consultants or by in-house people trained to teach the continuous improvement system. Most organizations that offer seminars can also help train people to give in-house education and training. To enhance in-house programs, videos describing the entire process and various phases of it are available. These videos can support and extend in-house teaching capability.

A Typical Education and Training Schedule

A typical schedule for an organization of 1,000 employees might look as follows:

Month 1—The chief executive (or division or department head), those reporting to him or her, and the people who will help implement the system read one or more books on the subject.

Month 2—These same people attend a public seminar. They learn the power of the continuous improvement system and talk to people from other companies in various stages of implementation.

Month 3—The group forms a steering committee to plan the transition and to insure that the necessary resources are made available.

Month 3-4—The committee formulates plans and schedules for the education and training programs, publicizes the organization's intent, requests volunteers to aid in the training, and screens the volunteers for degree of interest, background and teaching ability. These people can come from any level and any function. The volunteers need to understand that the training will be in addition to their regular duties. (Large organizations probably will have full-time trainers.) People who have received education should be starting simple projects in their own area. Move people into action as early as possible.

Month 5—The volunteers and selected managers begin attending the same public or private seminar attended by the others in month 2.

Months 5-6—Provide trainers with additional education in the basic tools of continuous improvement. The steering committee plans and tests internal training courses.

Month 6—Trainers, either employees or outside consultants, give abbreviated in-house educational seminars (6 to 8 hours) to all employees who have not attended an outside seminar. Management's support should be obvious.

Preferably the chief executive should introduce, attend, and make closing remarks at the seminar. This is a good time for the chief executive and/or other leaders to outline the reasons for the undertaking and the expected results. People will need to be convinced that this will be an enduring effort, not just another transitory "program."

Month 6-7—At all levels, groups identify projects and project teams for beginning efforts. The initial projects should be in significant areas, but should be reasonably simple ones, so that results can be seen in a relatively short period. Over the first few years of the new system, the number and scope of projects will build continuously.

Month 3-8—Training is underway and continues forever. By the end of year 1, some major projects are underway. Some organizations will be able to accomplish the above in less time.

The goal is to move successfully through Phase 1 - Building The Infrastructure and into Phase 2 - Running The Business. In Phase 2, companies experience quantum gains in quality reliability, costs, productivity, and customer satisfaction.

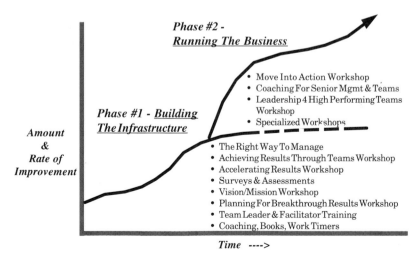

TRAINING

Some people will require more training than others, depending on their role. Train all employees in three areas—the simple tools, principles of work, and the human relations aspects of the continuous improvement process including teams and teamwork. Leaders of the continuous improvement effort need the training first. Although self-education is possible, it is probably more effective to have the leaders go to classes or workshops, either ones offered by a local university or those given by consultants specializing in this area. Besides these three subjects, people should be trained for the things they are likely to use. Do the training just before it is put to use. Training can also assist people in solving problems as they encounter them.

Provide a way for participants to evaluate the course. Feedback is useful in the continuous improvement of the course material and the trainers' abilities. Video courses can be quite valuable as a part of the training and for review. A selection of these courses is shown in Resources. Training, education, and learning are ongoing, never-ending processes.

The Simple Tools

Everyone needs to learn how to use the simple tools and when to use them. People also need to know how to gather data to use the tools effectively.

The best text I have found for this purpose is Ishikawa's *Guide to Quality Control.*[2] Cover the following chapters at a minimum.

Chapter 1—How to Collect Data
Chapter 2—Histograms
Chapter 3—Cause and Effect (Fishbone) Diagrams
Chapter 5—Pareto Diagrams
Chapter 9—Scatter Diagrams (Correlation Charts)

The only simple charts that Ishikawa's book does not adequately cover are the simple run chart and the flow chart. Outlines of these two tools are covered in *The Quality Secret*[3] on pages 63-68 and pages 88-95 respectively. Conway Quality's *Waste Chasers*[4] provides an explanation of how to use all these tools. More detail on flow charting is given on pages 174-180 of this book.

During this training emphasize practice problems. Chapter 13 of Ishikawa's book gives several practice problems.

The objective of this training is to have each participant understand when it is appropriate to use each of these charts, know how to gather data, and be able construct and interpret each type of chart. Place emphasis in each class on the types of charts that group is most likely to use. People should know how to use charts to help in improving processes.

At the end of this course, spend an hour on the principles of statistical control charts. People should understand how a control chart can be used to stabilize, improve, and control a process, but at this point not everyone needs to understand the theoretical basis of a control chart or how to construct one. Control charts are particularly important for people responsible for, or involved in, repetitive operations.

Principles of Work and Waste

Another course should cover the concepts of work, work processes, and the use of basic industrial engineering tools which are used to discover the waste. Key areas are: understanding that almost all waste is caused by the systems and processes of work, understanding value-added work, categorizing work, work sampling, and work analysis. These subjects are all designed to help understand what work is being done, what part of the work is value-added, and how it can be improved. This material is covered in Chapters 2 and 3 of *The Quality Secret*. During the course, assign each person to sample and categorize his or her own work. This is the best way to convince people how much waste there is in the work being done.

The course should cover basic industrial engineering tools such as work simplification and methods analysis. Also, a methodology for solving problems and a structured way of asking questions about the work are valuable. These are covered in *The Quality Secret.*

Human Relations

Probably the most important part of Human Relations is the education of top and senior management and their subsequent action to change the Human Relations, Education, Communications and other systems to lift all the people up (make them more capable) and make it in their interest to participate actively both individually and collectively in Continuous Improvement. They will usually need courses adapted for their education, as well as continued coaching by a competent consultant over a period of several years.

Course Objectives. The major objectives of the human relations course are to:

- Teach people how to show respect for other's ideas
- Train people to work together in teams
- Teach listening and communication skills
- Develop enthusiasm for the process of continuous improvement
- Unearth practices that are bothering people
- Communicate how the organization intends to operate.

One of the key points taught by Dr. Deming is that the people operating a process are the "experts." They know the most about how the process actually operates, what things go wrong, and where to find the waste. Human relations in the process of continuous improvement are built around this concept. Workers should lead, not follow, and they need to communicate their expert knowledge to others working in the same process and people from outside the process who can help them. Ideally, the people operating a process should work as a team to find the waste and bring about continuous improvement.

The scope of human relations training will depend heavily on the culture and history of each organization. Some will accept a new system fairly readily if they trust the fairness and competence of management. Where there has been a history of mistrust, words will not suffice to change attitudes. People will look on new management initiatives with skepticism and anxiety. Management will have to show by its actions that it treats people and their ideas with respect. Managers working to build trust should state their intentions only to the extent that they are sure they can fulfill them. Then they should ensure the intentions are followed.

Course Content. COMMUNICATION AND TEAM-WORK—There are many books and sources to teach listening and communications skills. A favorite is the classic by Dale Carnegie,[5] which emphasizes respect for people and the golden rule of human relations, to treat others as you would like to be treated. People need to respect each other before they can communicate effectively.

MUTUAL RESPECT is also necessary for working in teams. Team projects are a critical element of the continuous improvement system, so helping people to work as a team is vital. Often, working together in a class can begin the process of team building. A good background book is Joiner Associates' *Team Handbook.*[6]

Topics covered in training for teamwork should include:

- Forming a team
- Team dynamics
- Listening and communicating
- Effective meetings
- Team goals
- Decision procedures
- Documenting progress

Those people chosen as facilitators or team leaders will need additional training. These courses are available from Conway

Quality Inc. and others. Topics to be covered include

- Role of the facilitator, team leader, time keeper, scribe and team sponsor
- Managing meetings
- Establishing values and guidelines
- Effective communication
- Managing conflict
- Identifying and quantifying waste
- Building effective teams
- Education and training issues

One session should deal with CUSTOMER AND SUPPLIER RELATIONSHIPS. This should include a through discussion of the Interfaces, Interstices and Boundaries as discussed on page 60. The primacy of pleasing the external customer is a key element in continuous improvement. Involving suppliers and customers (internal and/or external) as part of a team greatly enhances the effort to improve a process. Identify the internal and external customers. Listen to and communicate with customers and suppliers to understand each other's needs. Determine how work for internal customers satisfies needs of external customers.

The instruction in human relations offers an opportunity for management to listen to and communicate with the organization. We find it useful to hold occasional "venting" sessions, during which people can vent their gripes, fears and frustrations about their work and the organization. Every attempt should be made to keep these sessions constructive, without finger-pointing and name-calling. People should understand that management will listen, but cannot respond to petty gripes. A follow-up venting session about six weeks after the first one is useful to determine how people have modified their thinking. We have found that when people are working in continuous improvement with the active involvement of management, their attitudes toward their organization and managers significantly improve.

Imagineering. People should understand what imagineering is and why it is so powerful.   They should know how to use it to release innovation and creativity.

One good way of keeping a venting session positive is to ask people to imagineer their job situation. What would their job be like if everything were perfect—no troubles, problems or waste? This question helps convert criticism into a search for improvement.

KEEP COURSES FLEXIBLE

Do not teach all tools and concepts to everyone initially. Review the course material for what will be useful to the group involved. Including a number of things not likely to be used will blur the focus on the more important subjects, and tools not used will be forgotten. If a course is abbreviated, additional written and/or video material should be available to those who request it. Some people will want to learn as much as they can. Encourage them!

Those who have had all the training outlined above should understand:

1. How to gather data and use check sheets and the six basic charts;
2. The principles and purpose of statistical control and when to consider the use of control charts;
3. The concept of value-added work;
4. The basic industrial engineering tools—work sampling, process flow charts, work simplification and methods analysis—and how to use them;
5. Imagineering;
6. The concepts that should govern relationships with customers and suppliers and how to use these concepts in their own work and that of their unit;
7. The importance of continuous process improvement;
8. The "Golden Rule" of human relations;

9. The importance of listening and communicating;
10. Why teamwork is important;
11. The benefits of personal satisfaction and increased competitiveness that come from practicing continuous improvement.

EXTRA TRAINING FOR SUPERVISORS, ENGINEERS, MANAGERS

People responsible for training, consulting and/or directing the activities of others in continuous improvement should have additional training and skills. They should:

1. Be able to use statistical control charts in simple applications
2. Demonstrate more advanced knowledge of industrial engineering tools and principles so that they can teach others
3. Understand and use process improvement methodology
4. Develop more advanced knowledge of the four forms of waste and practice finding them
5. Understand why it is usually good to reduce the number of suppliers
6. Understand and be able to teach the principles of customer and supplier relationships. Be able to work with customers and suppliers to show them the value and methods of cooperation
7. Understand and teach the "model"
8. Identify and develop key measurements for their business unit and its work processes
9. Undergo training in leadership and team building
10. Understand and use the five process checks for human relations
11. Undergo special training for working with unions, if the organization has unions

12. Attend additional training sessions in the concepts of value-added work, measurement, imagineering and just-in-time

SELECTED ADVANCED TRAINING

Depending upon the phase of the effort and the degree of involvement, some participants will benefit from more advanced training in such subjects as:

- Advanced statistical control
- The uses for designed experiments
- Theory and techniques of performing designed experiments
- Quality function deployment
- Performance appraisals and reward systems
- Establishing mission and vision
- Quality planning
- Identifying waste

INFRASTRUCTURE FOR TRAINING

With so much material to be covered, and with normal turnover of personnel, plan for a substantial, continuing training effort. Smaller companies can accomplish this goal with a combination of part-time, in-house trainers, outside consultants, and seminars or courses given by outsiders. One person should have the overall responsibility for training for continuous improvement. That person's responsibilities include assessing training needs, evaluating sources of training, recommending programs, and performing follow-up assessments of training effectiveness. Training resources include:

- Internal personnel acting as trainers
- Books and other literature

- Video courses with leader's delivery kits
- Seminars offered by consultants
- Courses given by area colleges, if available

Training of internal trainers may pose a problem for the smaller company. Anyone chosen should have good communication skills, be enthusiastic, and be willing to spend extra time learning the concepts and tools to be taught.

Larger organizations will want to develop more in-house training capability, with people serving full-time as trainers, facilitators and consultants. At Nashua Corporation, with about 4,000 USA employees, we had 3 full-time trainers/facilitators in addition to 5 or 6 part-time instructors. Also, in order to supplement the work of Dr. Deming, we hired Dr. Lloyd Nelson, a prominent statistician, to provide advice and counsel to project teams, and to help train and supervise the trainers. Dr. Nelson reported directly to me as CEO which gave him access to the resources needed. It also sent a signal to the organization as to the importance of understanding and using statistical variation to discover and eliminate waste.

Trainers can act as facilitators for project teams. They can attend team meetings, answer questions about using the tools, and insure that the team maintains focus on significant problems and/or opportunities. Sometimes teams get bogged down in minutiae of no real significance to continuous improvement. At other times teams substantially finish a worthwhile project but then continue to work on it, when they should find new projects or be disbanded.

APPENDIX D
Using Random Work Sampling

Work Sampling

Work sampling can be used by everyone at every level of the organization. It uses a large number of random samples of the work processes of people or machines to provide more accurate information about where time is being spent. And it identifies more waste. It is relatively easy to do and to train people to do. It is inexpensive. Everyone can participate, and teams from different levels can work together.

Principles of work sampling—The principles of work sampling are fairly simple. First, make the observations at random times. If you take an observation at 10:05 every day, and that was when the group was on break, you would get a false measurement of the time spent on breaks.

Second, you need have a large number of observations. If a person or group works on many activities, then you need more observations for a given level of accuracy. Suppose that you are walking down the street and the first man you see has a beard. Can you conclude that all men in that town have beards? Not from a sample of one. Suppose that the next five men you see do not have beards. Can you conclude that one out of six men have beards? Not with any degree of assurance. Suppose you walk down various streets in the area several times each day at various times for a month, make 500+ observations, and find that one out of every three men observed has a beard. Then you can conclude, with reasonable accuracy, that one-third of the men in that area have beards, because you have a reasonably large number of samples from which to draw a conclusion. What you're really talking about is probability. You think there's a good probability that about one-third of the men have beards. You've made enough observations over a long enough period to give you a feeling of confidence in your prediction.

Third, observations should be made over a complete cycle. Many work activities occur in cycles. For example, shipments and billings may be heavy at the end of the month. People who close the books each month do quite different things the first several days after the end of the month than they do for the rest of the month. Even people who do the same thing every day may do different things in the early morning than they do the rest of the day. In this case cover the full day to complete the cycle. Repeat the sampling for four or five days to make sure you get a representative sample and that you have enough observations.

How many observations do you need to obtain a reasonable degree of accuracy? Sampling even the simplest, most repetitive work requires at least 100 samples. The more diverse the activities, and the longer the cycle, the more observations you need. If work is done on a weekly cycle, you need more observations than for a daily cycle—a rule of thumb is at least 300 observations. When the work is on a monthly cycle, you'll need at least 550. The other factor that affects the number of observations needed is the diversity of the job. If you have a job that has 20 different activities, then you will need more observations than if you have 5 activities. The table below will give you an idea of how many samples you need depending on the diversity of the work. The accuracy of any sample will be less for those activities occupying a small percentage of your time than for major activities. It is the major uses of time you want to study closely.

Observations Required Chart

Estimated % Occurrence of Activity	68% Confidence ±10%	95% Confidence ±10%	99% Confidence ±10%
15	567	2270	5100
20	400	1600	3600
25	300	1200	2700
30	233	935	2100
35	186	745	1670
40	150	600	1350
45	122	490	1100
50	100		

These numbers have been derived from mathematical formula per Motion and Time Study Design and Measurement of Work, 7th edition, Ralph M. Barnes, Author, 1980 John Wiley & Sons, Inc.

State the problem. The purpose of your initial studies will be to find out what work is being done and to classify it in categories to enable you to find and eliminate the waste. In the future, the work sampling studies you do may attack very specific problems.

Decide what information is needed and how the activities should be classified. Make a list of all the activities in your unit that you can think of and decide how fine a breakdown will be useful for you. Then classify them into the five types of work: value-added, necessary, rework, other unnecessary work, and time not working.

Determine the scope of the study. To start, you usually study all operations. In some cases, if you have a large number of people doing the same things, you may be able to select a representative few to give you data which will be accurate enough for the whole group. In general, unless you have ten or more people doing the same job, it is best to have everyone participate in the study.

Ensure employee awareness of the study, its goals and benefits. Explain the reasons for the study to all participants and tell them how the data will to be used: by management to find ways to improve the system and eliminate external and internal problems; and by the people doing the work to make improvements and changes in areas over which they have power. Then get the facts so they can act. We are trying to make each person's job easier so that he or she can better utilize time, energy, and brain power on value-added work. No one likes to work on things that are a waste of time. We're not trying to get greater effort from anybody provided that effort is now reasonable, we're just trying to insure that that effort is on the right things, and done without waste.

Plan the study. First make a list of activities to track. Obtain this from the list of activities on the running work record. Again, don't list any activity separately if it looks as though it will take less than 3% of the total time. Try to combine that activity with some companion activity.

Prepare a work analysis and observation form like the one shown in Chapter 7. The headings of this form list the five categories of work. Under each heading is room for listing a number of activities. If a person has too many activities to fit on one form, use two forms, or shrink some of the work classification headings and expand others. Each person can make a check mark in the column showing what activity he or she is doing whenever a random time signal is heard. How do you get this random time signal? Random electronic timers are available[1], which can be set for an average frequency of signals per day. They will sound a buzzer or make a pulse signal at frequencies between five and 64 times per 8 hour day. You will probably want to average between twenty and twenty-five samples a day. This allows people to gather samples reasonably quickly, without disrupting their train of thought too often.

You will need a daily copy of the work analysis and observation form with the activities filled in for each person. Following is a sample.

Total Obs.	Observations (Check Appropriate Work Activity)	Specific Work Activity		
		Word Processing	Value Added Work	Categories of Work
		Copying		
		Binding		
		Maintain Mailing Lists		
		Receive Fax		
		Send Fax		
		Label & File Diskettes	Necessary Work (Non-Value Added)	
		Answer Phone		
		Call Customer To Advise Work Done		
		Change Copier/ Printer Supplies		
		Attend Meetings		
		Make Minor Changes	Unnecessary Work (Rework)	
		Make Major Changes		
		Resend Fax		
		Call For Service/Repair	Unnecessary Work (All Other)	
		Call Customer To Clarify Work		
		Daily Reports		
		Breaks	Not Working Authorized	
		Wait Supplies		
		Wait Service Repair		
		Idle - No Work		
		Talking	Not Working Not Auth.	
		Time of Observation		

Position: _____   Name: _____   Date: _____

WorkTime Analyzer©

As you can see, the activities are grouped under the five categories of work, so you can make a Pareto chart of the overall categories.

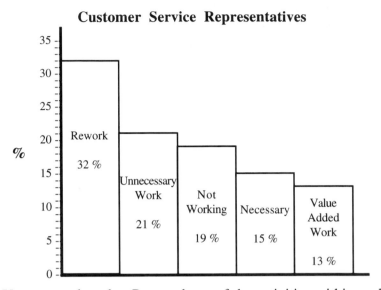

Customer Service Representatives

You can make other Pareto charts of the activities within each category. Pareto charts of the wasteful activities, such as the rework and the unnecessary work, are particularly important. A sample Pareto chart of rework is shown below.

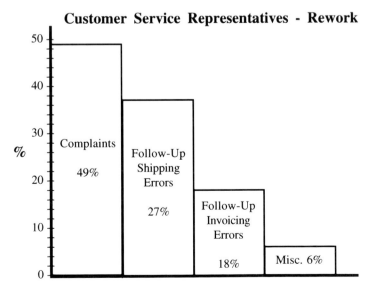

Customer Service Representatives - Rework

The Pareto chart helps you decide what to work on first to eliminate the most waste. In this case you can see that 32% of the work consists of rework or other unnecessary work! This provides a great opportunity for finding ways to eliminate that waste.

Usually start with the biggest source of waste, but not always. You may want to start with the waste that is most important to the external customer, most important to employees, involves the largest amount of money, can be done quickly, etc.

APPENDIX E
Practice Flow Chart

The purpose of this exercise is to give you some practice in making a flow chart. It's a simple case, but typical of many work areas. We will describe the first five steps in making the chart and ask you to complete the next five steps. The list of steps is repeated here for your convenience.

 Decide what process to improve. Describe the value added products and services produced by that process.

 Give the process a title.

 Gain knowledge and understanding of the work being done. This is a necessary preliminary step to flow charting. Discuss all assumed sub-activities with the people doing the work.

 Identify the suppliers and customers of the work process. Give the specific inputs and outputs related to each. (Flow charts should show suppliers on the left, the work process in the center, and its customers on the right.)

 Decide on detail of process flow chart. Write an initial description of each step in the process. This helps us understand just what goes into each step, and often reveals complexities and problems as we examine our results.

 Observe and record the actual activities using the process flow chart data sheets (Appendix A). Include times for each step.

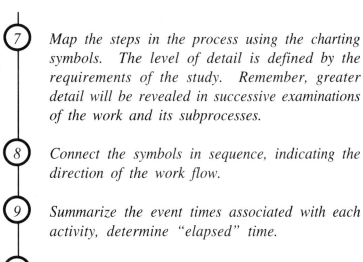

7 *Map the steps in the process using the charting symbols.   The level of detail is defined by the requirements of the study.   Remember, greater detail will be revealed in successive examinations of the work and its subprocesses.*

8 *Connect the symbols in sequence, indicating the direction of the work flow.*

9 *Summarize the event times associated with each activity, determine "elapsed" time.*

10 *Produce Pareto charts of all times by category. This allows us to see where the time is being spent. Simply by adding the times by symbol we know how much time in the process goes into transport, inspection, decision-making, operations, and delay.   This knowledge gives us a clear direction towards improving the work process.*

This case is about a customer service department.

The first step is to decide what to work on. This department had a write up of their activities and completed some preliminary work to tell them what time was spent on each activity. They found their biggest single problem area was handling pricing complaints from their external customers. In fact, they found that of the five account representatives spent 7.5% of their time just working on those external customer complaints due to pricing. Since this is not value-added work, the department supervisor asked her boss to start a project to get rid of pricing complaints. Her boss agreed to begin a project but wanted the customer service group to flow chart their activities in responding to customer complaints.

Step 2 is to give the process a title. They selected, "Handling Customer Complaints on Pricing."

In Step 3, the person in charge of the study must get a good grasp of the work. In this case, that person is the customer service manager. She talked with all the people who work on the complaints in her department, with her suppliers of information, and with her internal customers and some of her external customers. She got them all involved in helping her to understand the process. At the same time, she let them know what she was doing and asked for their cooperation.

In Step 4, she identified the suppliers and customers of the process. The suppliers are those people who provide information about the pricing complaint. In this case, the external customer is also a supplier, since the customer supplies information. Other suppliers are the central file group and the sales department. The work unit processes the information and their product is a resolved complaint. So a better title might be "Resolving Customer Pricing Complaints."

Think in terms of the product or service you are providing. In this case the external customer is both a supplier and a customer. He supplies you with an unresolved complaint; you process that complaint and in turn give him your product, which is a resolved complaint.

Step 5 is to take what you have learned and start to map the work, how it is presently being done. This list is the result of all the discussions the manager has had with the people working for her and with her suppliers and customers. She started with a preliminary list and then got more ideas from discussing the list.

Now you are ready to go to work. Since you're not in a position to gather all the facts in this case, we have provided the information—maybe not in the detail that you'd like, but enough for you to make a flow chart. The description is on page 233. A word of caution: there may be more than one type of task included in the description of each action. For example, one of the actions states that the account representative "goes to copy machine, waits for copier to warm up and makes copies." Actually, there are three types of tasks involved in this action. Walking to the copying machine is a movement or transfer, which will be represented by an arrow, waiting for the machine to warm up is a delay, represented by a 'D', and making the copies is an operation, a circle. When reading the description of what the person does, break it down into its elements. In analyzing the work, you might decide that making copies is absolutely necessary, and if you describe the task as just making copies, you might look no further. But, if you list the transport and delay separately, it would lead you to look at possible relocation of the copy machine, and leaving it on during the work day to avoid waiting for it to warm up.

Step 6 includes writing a description of each task along with the time taken at each step. Look at the description of the process on page 233, and using the blank form on page 235, write a description of each of the tasks in sequence. In this case, we have given you no information about times, so you can make a rough estimate of how long you think it would take to do each task. Obviously there is no right or wrong on the times in this case, so just estimate the time.

For Step 7, fill in the appropriate symbol beside each task. For review, the symbols mean as follows:

Symbols		Denotes	Examples
Diamond	◆	Decision	• is the part good? • is the supplier the right one?
Square	■	Control/ Inspection	• verify travel requisition • check time cards • inspect part • approve salary increase
Circle	●	Operation	• make a copy • type a memo • run a machine • interview applicant

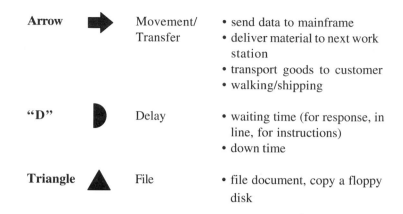

Arrow	Movement/ Transfer	• send data to mainframe • deliver material to next work station • transport goods to customer • walking/shipping
"D"	Delay	• waiting time (for response, in line, for instructions) • down time
Triangle	File	• file document, copy a floppy disk

There may be some gray areas in this step such as whether getting a form from the drawer is a delay or a movement. Don't worry about the gray areas. Just pick the symbol that best describes the task to you.

Next, in step 8, connect the symbols you have picked for each task by drawing straight lines between them in sequence. In this case the account representative is the only one involved in the tasks shown, but in other activities you will have more than one person and maybe more than one department involved.

After connecting the tasks in sequence, go to step 9, which is adding the times for all the operations type tasks, the delays, the decisions, and so forth. This will give you an idea of how much time is spent in the various activities. Add the grand total of the elapsed time for the whole process.

Step 10 is to take the times of each type of task, such as delays, operations, etc., and make a Pareto chart, of all the six types of tasks in descending order of time. This should give you a good feel as to where some of the waste is and how much time is spent on non-productive tasks such as delays and transports.

The data collection sheet, as I filled it out, is on page 235-236 and is followed by the Pareto chart. Compare the two without worrying about differences in time estimates.

What can you learn from the exercise? What more data do you need? Where could improvements be made? What should you work on first? Second? Breaking down the tasks and the work flow like this is a critical step in locating the waste.

Handling Customer Complaints on Pricing

— Description of Process

The account representative (A/R Rep) answers the phone and determines by talking with the customer that the customer has a pricing complaint. The representative obtains a standard complaint form from the bottom drawer and, through further discussion with the customer, understands and records the complaint on the form. At the end of the conversation, the rep advises the customer that his/her complaint will receive immediate attention and that a follow-up call will be made to ensure the customer's satisfaction with the outcome. The rep then goes to the central invoice file on the third floor. (The rep's department is on the first floor.) The rep searches for the invoice but does not find it in the files. The rep then goes to the central file 'in' basket, searches for and finds the invoice. The rep then returns to desk with the invoice. The rep removes the price book from the shelf, searches for the correct page, and determines if the complaint is valid. The rep obtains a credit form from desk drawer and prepares the credit form. The rep goes to the copy machine, waits for the copier to warm up and makes two copies of the invoice and one copy each of the complaint and the credit form. The rep then returns to the work station and files the forms in a pending file. The rep then returns to the elevator, takes the invoice to the central file 'in' basket on the third floor and returns to his/her desk. The rep later receives a copy of the credit invoice and retrieves documents from the pending file. The rep calls the customer to advise that the credit has been approved. The rep destroys the pending file copies. The rep takes the credit invoice to central files, searches for and finds the original invoice. The rep then staples the credit invoice to the original invoice. The rep goes to the central file 'in' basket and puts the document in the 'in' basket. The rep returns to his/her desk.

Process Flow Chart Data Collection　　　☐　Present Method　　　☐　Proposed Method

Subject Charted _____　　　Date _____

_____　　　Chart by _____

_____　　　Chart # _____

Department _____　　　Sheet #_____ of _____

Time In Seconds	Chart Symbols	Process Description
	○ ⇨ ☐ ◇ D ▽	
	○ ⇨ ☐ ◇ D ▽	
	○ ⇨ ☐ ◇ D ▽	
	○ ⇨ ☐ ◇ D ▽	
	○ ⇨ ☐ ◇ D ▽	
	○ ⇨ ☐ ◇ D ▽	
	○ ⇨ ☐ ◇ D ▽	
	○ ⇨ ☐ ◇ D ▽	
	○ ⇨ ☐ ◇ D ▽	
	○ ⇨ ☐ ◇ D ▽	
	○ ⇨ ☐ ◇ D ▽	
	○ ⇨ ☐ ◇ D ▽	
	○ ⇨ ☐ ◇ D ▽	
	○ ⇨ ☐ ◇ D ▽	
	○ ⇨ ☐ ◇ D ▽	
	○ ⇨ ☐ ◇ D ▽	
	○ ⇨ ☐ ◇ D ▽	
	○ ⇨ ☐ ◇ D ▽	
	○ ⇨ ☐ ◇ D ▽	
	○ ⇨ ☐ ◇ D ▽	
	○ ⇨ ☐ ◇ D ▽	
	○ ⇨ ☐ ◇ D ▽	
	○ ⇨ ☐ ◇ D ▽	
	○ ⇨ ☐ ◇ D ▽	

Process Flow Chart Data Collection   ☒ Present Method   ☐ Proposed Method

Subject Charted _Handling Customer Complaints On Pricing_   Date   _10/31_

_____   Chart by _LCH_

_____   Chart # _101_

Department _____   Sheet # _1_ of _2_

Time In Seconds	Chart Symbols	Process Description
10	● ⇨ □ ◇ D ▽	Answer phones
20	○ ⇨ □ ◆ D ▽	Determine nature of complaint
5	○ ➡ □ ◇ D ▽	Obtain complaint form
40	○ ⇨ ■ ◇ D ▽	Understand & record complaint
15	● ⇨ □ ◇ D ▽	Advise customer of call back
120	○ ➡ □ ◇ D ▽	Go to central files
150	○ ⇨ □ ◇ D ▼	Search for invoice
60	○ ⇨ □ ◇ D ▼	Search central file in-basket
120	○ ➡ □ ◇ D ▽	Return to desk
5	○ ➡ □ ◇ D ▽	Obtain price book
10	● ⇨ □ ◇ D ▽	Search for right page
30	○ ⇨ □ ◆ D ▽	Determine validity of complaint
10	○ ➡ □ ◇ D ▽	Obtain credit form
90	● ⇨ □ ◇ D ▽	Prepare credit form
110	○ ➡ □ ◇ D ▽	Go to copy machine
30	○ ⇨ □ ◇ ◗ ▽	Wait for copy machine to warm up
30	● ⇨ □ ◇ D ▽	Make copies
40	○ ➡ □ ◇ D ▽	Return to work station
15	○ ⇨ □ ◇ D ▼	File forms in pending file
120	○ ➡ □ ◇ D ▽	Go to central files
5	○ ⇨ □ ◇ D ▼	Leave invoice in in-basket
120	○ ➡ □ ◇ D ▽	Return to desk
10	● ⇨ □ ◇ D ▽	Receive copy of credit
45	○ ⇨ □ ◇ D ▼	Retrieve documents from file

Process Flow Chart Data Collection   ☒ Present Method   ☐ Proposed Method

Subject Charted _Handling Customer Complaints On Pricing_   Date _10/31_

_____   Chart by _LCH_

_____   Chart # _101_

Department _____   Sheet #_ 2 _ of _ 2 _

Time In Seconds	Chart Symbols	Process Description
60	● ⇨ ☐ ◇ D ▽	Call customer with credit advice
10	○ ⇨ ☐ ◇ D ▼	Destroy file copies
120	○ ➡ ☐ ◇ D ▽	Take credit invoice to central file
50	○ ⇨ ☐ ◇ D ▼	Find original invoice
10	● ⇨ ☐ ◇ D ▽	Staple credit to original invoice
20	○ ➡ ☐ ◇ D ▽	Go to central file in-basket
5	○ ⇨ ☐ ◇ D ▼	Put document in basket
120	○ ➡ ☐ ◇ D ▽	Return to desk
	○ ⇨ ☐ ◇ D ▽	
	○ ⇨ ☐ ◇ D ▽	
	○ ⇨ ☐ ◇ D ▽	
	○ ⇨ ☐ ◇ D ▽	
	○ ⇨ ☐ ◇ D ▽	
	○ ⇨ ☐ ◇ D ▽	
	○ ⇨ ☐ ◇ D ▽	
	○ ⇨ ☐ ◇ D ▽	
	○ ⇨ ☐ ◇ D ▽	
	○ ⇨ ☐ ◇ D ▽	
	○ ⇨ ☐ ◇ D ▽	
	○ ⇨ ☐ ◇ D ▽	
	○ ⇨ ☐ ◇ D ▽	
	○ ⇨ ☐ ◇ D ▽	
	○ ⇨ ☐ ◇ D ▽	
	○ ⇨ ☐ ◇ D ▽	

Categories Of Activities & Tasks

VA	Value Added
N	Necessary
RW	Rework
UN	Unnecessary
NW	Not Working
II	Insufficient Info

N	Fill out expense report
RW	Approve expense report of subordinate
UN	Provide second approval of expense report
N/UN	Audit approved expense report
N	Pay reimbursement of expenses
VA	Prepare for sales call on potential customer
VA	Make sales call on potential customer
VA	Make phone calls to get appointments with potential customers
N	Travel to present customer's office
VA/UN	Take customer to lunch
VA/UN	Play golf with customer
VA	Present new product information to customer
VA	Take order from customer
N/RW	Ask customer to pay overdue invoice
N	Resolve customer quality complaint
RW	Explain billing error to customer
VA	Explain forthcoming price increase to customer
N/UN	Prepare journal entry for monthly closing
N/UN	Compute standard cost variances
N	Prepare monthly profit and loss statement
N/UN	Print and distribute monthly accounting reports
N	Prepare annual budget
RW	Correct mistaken accounting entry
N/UN	Take physical inventory
N	Prepare sales tax return
RW	File amended tax return
N	Talk to supervisor about your health problem and absenteeism
N/II	Talk to supervisor about your new baby
II	Talk to fellow employee about your new baby
II	Talk to fellow employee about your health problem
II	Talk to supervisor about ball game
II	Take a sick day because you deserve it
VA/RW	Discuss errors with another department with supervisor
N	Correct errors made by another department
RW	Prepare a report on last month's shipping errors
RW	Prepare a report on last year's shipping errors
VA/RW	Prepare a report on today's shipping errors
VA/RW	Keep a run chart on level of unresolved customer complaints
VA	Make a Pareto chart of reasons for claims
N	Prepare a weekly payroll
N/UN	Write weekly payroll checks
N/UN	Distribute weekly payroll checks
II	Cash weekly payroll checks
RW	Prepare a report which no one uses to make a decision or take action

VA/UN   Prepare a report of sales by product line

II   Make copies on copy machine

NW   Wait in line at copy machine

N/UN   File last years sales reports

N   File last years tax return

Notes

[1] For information, call Conway Quality, Inc.: 1-800-359-0099

[2] Ishikawa, *Guide to Quality Control*, UNIPUB, Box 433 Murray Hill Station, NY, NY 10157. 800-521-8110

[3] William Conway, *The Quality Secret*, Conway Quality, Inc., 15 Trafalgar Square, Nashua, NH 03063. 800-359-0099.

[4] William Conway, *Waste Chasers*, Conway Quality, Inc., 15 Trafalgar Square, Nashua, NH 03063. 800-359-0099

[5] *How to Win Friends and Influence People*, Dale Carnegie. Simon and Schuster, Inc., 1230 Avenue of the Americas, New York, NY 10020.

[6] *The Team Handbook*, Joiner Associates, Inc., 3800 Regent Street, Madison, WI 53705-0445. 608-238-8134.

RESOURCES

Dr. Deming/Deming Philosophy

Out of the Crisis
W. Edwards Deming. Massachusetts Institute of
Technology, Center for Advanced Engineering Study,
Cambridge, MA 02139. 1986. Telephone 617-253-7444.

The New Economics
W. Edwards Deming. Massachusetts Institute of
Technology, Center for Advanced Engineering Study,
Cambridge, MA 02139. 1993. Telephone 617-253-7444.

The Deming Management Method
Mary Walton. Putnam Publishing Group, 200 Madison
Avenue, NY, NY 10016.

The Deming Dimension
Henry Neave, Ph.D., SPC Press, Inc., 5908 Toole Drive,
Suite C, Knoxville, TN 37919. Telephone 615-584-5005.

Deming's Road To Continual Improvement
William W. Scherkenbach. Mercury Press/Fairchild
Publications, Rockville, MD 20852. Telephone 301-770-
6177.

The Deming Route to Quality and Productivity
William W. Scherkenbach. Mercury Press/Fairchild
Publications, Rockville, MD 20852. Telephone 301-770-
6177.

Total Quality Management/Continuous Improvement

The Quality Secret: The Right Way To Manage©
William E. Conway. Conway Quality, Inc., 15 Trafalgar
Square, Nashua, NH 03063. Telephone 800-359-0099.
Fax 603-889-0033.

Guide to Quality Control
Ishikawa. UNIPUB. Box 433, Murray Hill Station, NY, NY
10157. Telephone 800-521-8110.

What is Total Quality Control?
Ishikawa. UNIPUB. Box 433, Murray Hill Station, NY, NY
10157. Telephone 800-521-8110.

Understanding Variation: The Key To Managing Chaos
Donald J. Wheeler, SPC Press, Inc., 5908 Toole Drive,
Suite C, Knoxville, TN 37919. Telephone 615-584-5005.

Quality Planning and Analysis
Juran/Gryna. Second Edition. McGraw-Hill Book
Company, New York, NY. Telephone 212-512-2000.

Quality or Else
Lloyd Dobyns & Clare Crawford-Mason. Houghton Mifflin
Company, 2 Park Street, Boston, MA 02108. Telephone
617-725-5000.

The Art of Japanese Management
Richard Tanner Pascale & Anthony G. Athos. Warner
Books, New York, NY

Commit to Quality
Patrick L. Townsend & Joan E. Gebhardt. John Wiley &
Sons, Inc. 605 3rd Avenue, New York, NY 10158-0012.
Telephone 212-850-6418.

Toyota Production System/J-I-T

Toyota Production System
Taiichi Ohno. Productivity Press, Inc. P. O. Box 3007,
Dept 721, Cambridge, MA 02140. Telephone 800-274-
9911 (in Massachusetts 617-497-5146)

Workplace Management
Taiichi Ohno. Productivity Press, Inc. P. O. Box 3007,
Dept 721, Cambridge, MA 02140. Telephone 800-274-
9911 (in Massachusetts 617-497-5146)

Just-In-Time for Today and Tomorrow
Taiichi Ohno with Setsuo Mito. Productivity Press, Inc. P.
O. Box 3007, Dept 721, Cambridge, MA 02140. Telephone
800-274-9911 (in Massachusetts 617-497-5146)

Non-Stock Production
Shigeo Shingo. Productivity Press, Inc. P. O. Box 3007,
Dept 721, Cambridge, MA 02140. Telephone 800-274-
9911 (in Massachusetts 617-497-5146)

The Just-in-Time Breakthrough
Edward J. Hay. John Wiley & Sons, Inc. 605 3rd Avenue,
New York, NY 10158-0012. Telephone 212-850-6418.

World Class Manufacturing
Richard J. Schonberger. Free Press. 866 Third Avenue,
NY, NY 10022. Telephone 212-702-2000.

Case Studies/Stories

Deming Management at Work
Mary Walton. Putnam Publishing Group, 200 Madison
Avenue, NY, NY 10016.

Everyday Heroes
SPC Press, Inc., 5908 Toole Drive, Suite C, Knoxville, TN
37919. Telephone 615-584-5005.

Real People, Real Work
Lee Cheaney, Maury Cotter. SPC Press, Inc., 5908 Toole
Drive, Suite C, Knoxville, TN 37919. Telephone 615-584-
5005.

World Class Manufacturing Casebook
Richard J. Schonberger. Free Press. 866 Third Avenue,
NY, NY 10022. Telephone 212-702-2000.

The Goal
Eliyahu M. Goldratt and Jeff Cox. North River Press, Inc.
1986. Box 309 Croton-on-Hudson, NY 10520. Telephone
914-941-7175.

Customers

Building a Chain of Customers
Richard J. Schonberger. Free Press. 866 Third Avenue,
NY, NY 10022. Telephone 212-702-2000.

Tools

*Waste Chasers - A Pocket Guide to Quality and
Productivity*
Conway Quality, Inc., 15 Trafalgar Square, Nashua, NH
03063. Telephone 800-359-0099. Fax 603-889-0033.

SPC Simplified
Robert T. Amsden, Howard E. Butler, David M.
Amsden. UNIPUB, 1986. Kraus International Publications,
White Plains, NY.

SPC Simplified for Services
Robert T. Amsden, Howard E. Butler, David M. Amsden.
UNIPUB, 1986. Kraus International Publications, White
Plains, NY.

Teamwork/Teams/Empowerment

The Team Handbook
Joiner Associates, Inc., 3800 Regent Street, Madison, WI
53705-0445. Telephone 608-238-8134.

The Wisdom of Teams
Jon Katzenbach & Douglas Smith. Harvard Business
School Press, Boston MA. 1993

Team Players and Teamwork
Glenn M. Parker. Jossey-Bass, Inc. 350 Sansome Street,
San Francisco, CA 94104

Zapp
Robert W. Hall. Dow Jones-Irwin, Homewood, IL

How To Make Meetings Work
Michael Doyle, David Strauss. The Berkeley Publishing
Group, 200 Madison Avenue, New York, NY 10016

Games Trainers Play
John W. Newstorm & Edward E. Scannell, McGraw Hill,
1980. Telephone 212-512-2000

Leadership

A Force for Change
John P. Kotter. Free Press. 866 Third Avenue, NY, NY
10022. Telephone 212-702-2000

Principle Centered Leadership
Stephen R. Covey, Simon & Schuster, Inc. , New York

Flight of the Buffalo
James Belasco & Ralph Stayer. Warner Books, 1271
Avenue of the Americas, New York, NY 10070.

Juran on Quality Leadership
J. M. Juran. Free Press. 866 Third Avenue, NY, NY
10022. Telephone 212-702-2000

Human Relations

The 7 Habits of Highly Effective People
Stephen R. Covey, Simon & Schuster, Inc. , New York

Driving Fear Out Of The Workplace
Kathleen Ryan & Daniel Oestreich. Jossey-Bass, Inc. 350
Sansome Street, San Francisco, CA 94104.

No Contest: The Case Against Competition
Alfie Kohn, Houghton Mifflin Company, 2 Park Street,
Boston, MA 02108. Telephone 617-725-5000.

Employment Security in a Free Economy
Jerome Rostow. Pergamon Press. Elmsford, NY. Telephone
914-592-7700.

*Performance Appraisal: Perspectives on a Quality
Management Approach*
ASTD, 1630 Duke Street, Box 1443, Alexandria, VA
22313. Telephone 703-683-8100.

Periodicals

Quality Progress Magazine
American Society for Quality Control, 310 West Wisconsin Avenue, Milwaukee, WI 53203. Telephone 414-272-8575.

Training Magazine
Lakewood Publications, 50 South 9th Street, Minneapolis, MN 55402. Telephone 612-333-0471.

Harvard Business Review
Harvard Business Review, Boston, MA 02163. Telephone 1-800-274-3214.

Productivity, Inc. - **Newsletter**
Productivity Press, Inc. P. O. Box 3007, Dept 721, Cambridge, MA 02140. Telephone 800-274-9911 (in Massachusetts 617-497-5146)

INDEX